THE MEMOIRS OF WALTER BAGEHOT

FRANK PROCHASKA was born in America but has lived much of his life in England. His previous books include *Royal Bounty: The Making of a Welfare Monarchy* (1995) and *The Eagle and the Crown: Americans and the British Monarchy* (2008), both published by Yale University Press; *Women and Philanthropy in Nineteenth-Century England* (1980), *The Voluntary Impulse* (1988), *The Republic of Britain* (2000), *Christianity and Social Service in Modern Britain* (2006), and *Eminent Victorians on American Democracy* (2012). He has taught at universities on both sides of the Atlantic and in recent years taught British history at Yale. He has been a Visiting Fellow of All Souls College, Oxford and is an Honorary Fellow of the Institute of Historical Research, London University. He is currently a member of the History Faculty and of Somerville and Wolfson Colleges at the University of Oxford.

WALTER BAGEHOT

THE MEMOIRS OF
WALTER BAGEHOT

FRANK PROCHASKA

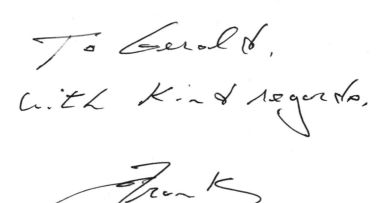

*To Gerald,
with kind regards,

Frank*

YALE UNIVERSITY PRESS
NEW HAVEN & LONDON

For information about this and other Yale University Press publications, please contact:
U.S. Office: sales.press@yale.edu   www.yalebooks.com
Europe Office: sales@yaleup.co.uk   www.yalebooks.co.uk

Set in Adobe Caslon Pro by IDSUK (DataConnection) Ltd
Printed in Great Britain by TJ International Ltd, Padstow, Cornwall

Library of Congress Cataloging-in-Publication Data

Prochaska, Frank
    The memoirs of Walter Bagehot / Frank Prochaska.
      pages cm
    ISBN 978-0-300-19554-5 (cl : alk. paper)
1. Bagehot, Walter, 1826–1877. 2. Great Britain—Politics and government—1837-1901. 3. Great Britain—Economic conditions—19th century. 4. Economists—Great Britain—Biography. 5. Journalists—Great Britain—Biography. 6. Intellectuals—Great Britain—Biography. I. Title.
    HB103.B2P76 2013
    330.092—dc23
    [B]
                                                                    2013010902

A catalogue record for this book is available from the British Library.

10 9 8 7 6 5 4 3 2 1

Contents

LIFT NOT THE PAINTED VEIL WHICH THOSE WHO LIVE
CALL LIFE.

Foreword

G. M. Young, the great historian of Victorian England, once turned over in his mind candidates for the title of the 'Greatest Victorian'. He was not looking for the supreme genius working in Britain between 1837 and 1901; if so, Darwin and George Eliot would have been among those with strong claims to the distinction. Instead, Young was looking for someone with a roomy and energetic mind, who could have been of no other time: 'a man with sympathy to share, and genius to judge, its sentiments and movements: a man not too illustrious or too consummate to be companionable, but one, nevertheless, whose ideas took root and are still bearing; whose influence, passing from one fit mind to another, could transmit, and can still impart, the most precious element in Victorian civilization, its robust and masculine sanity.' He awarded the title to Walter Bagehot.

I first discovered Bagehot through reading his *Historical Essays* as a student. Over the years, his works have played an increasing part in my own writings, particularly those on political thought and the British monarchy. In my last book, *Eminent Victorians on American Democracy*, I devoted a chapter to his criticism of the United States Constitution. As the manuscript was in production, I returned to some of his essays in *The Economist* and the *Saturday Review*, in which he dissected politics in a playful manner that made Victorian England seem timeless yet familiar. Sadly, he did not leave a memoir. Given my long-standing interest in his life and times I decided to compose one on his behalf. I chose to write the book in the first person because I thought Bagehot could speak more vividly of his life and mind than I could as an intermediary in a conventional biography.

Bagehot, to use his phrase, was a 'self-delineating' writer, someone who left a vibrant image of himself in his essays, books and letters. Much of the text that follows is in his own words, drawn from disparate sources, edited and expanded to create a life in narrative. Bagehot was a man of letters in the broadest sense, with an absorbent mind of remarkable versatility. Whatever he wrote – and he wrote brilliantly – he expressed in a lively, conversational style. Talking to him, said his friend William Roscoe, 'was like riding a horse with a perfect mouth'. His animated prose gives much the same pleasure, whether he was writing for leisured readers of the quarterlies or busy City men in *The Economist*. He delighted in aphorisms and despised what he saw as that most unpardonable of faults – dullness. If these memoirs are ever dull, the fault will be not Bagehot's but my own.

Unlike a conventional ghost writer, I have not been able to consult the subject in person. But I have sought to be sensitive to the way in which Bagehot would have portrayed himself had he left a memoir. On the surface, he was a man of buoyant cheerfulness, which disguised an underlying melancholic reserve. Well connected but with few intimate friends, he did not seek the limelight or push himself on others. On grounds of confidentiality, he would have understated his influence on government economic policy, which was not insignificant. He would also have been guarded about his personal and family life, as would have been usual in a mid-Victorian gentleman. In any case, there is nothing to suggest that he was anything but a dutiful son and a faithful husband. His mother, who suffered from mental illness, was the central character in his life, and he would have treated her with delicacy in a memoir. It seems unlikely that he would have discussed her descent into uncontrollable behaviour, which led to her incarceration in an asylum for several weeks in 1866.

Inevitably, a book of this hybrid nature is an historical reconstruction. Examples of the genre are rare, but splendidly achieved in Marguerite Yourcenar's *Memoirs of Hadrian*. As Yourcenar reminds us, the reconstruction of an historical figure written in the first person borders on fiction, but is greatly enriched by close adherence to the facts. Unlike Hadrian, Bagehot left a large body of material to draw on. His *Collected Works*, edited by Norman St John-Stevas, runs to fifteen volumes. In addition, there are the diaries of his wife Eliza, and various biographies, reviews and scholarly studies. Among the most helpful sources have been the 'Memoir' published in the *Fortnightly Review* (1877) by Richard Holt Hutton, the *Life of Walter Bagehot* (1914) by his sister-in-law Emilie Barrington, *The Love-letters of Walter Bagehot and Eliza Wilson* (1933), published by Mrs Barrington, *Walter Bagehot* (1939) by William Irvine, *The Spare Chancellor: The Life of Walter Bagehot* (1959) by Alastair Buchan, and *The Pursuit of Reason: The Economist 1843–1993* (1993) by Ruth Dudley Edwards.

Though this book is an historical reconstruction, it is also a literary exercise, which sanctions a degree of licence. Bagehot was a fine stylist, but when writing to deadlines he could be hasty and careless. To the dismay of his Victorian editors, he often wrote with scant regard for precision or proofreading. Consequently, I have amended his prose in places and have corrected his occasional misquotations, which resulted from his tendency to draw on his prodigious memory rather than published sources. All of the poetry quoted in these memoirs is either by Bagehot, cited by him or known to him. He did not often mention the names of the authors he cites, and I have largely kept to his practice. Where I have altered his writings and expanded the text to recreate his life, I have taken pains to avoid using words and phrases that he did not himself employ.

Of course, this is not the autobiography that Bagehot would have written had he left an autobiography; but it is, I believe, free of anachronism and true to his life and times. I have sought to be an amanuensis rather than a ventriloquist and throughout have tried to sustain his tone of voice and the flavour of his writing. I can only hope that Bagehot's shade would forgive the book's liberties, and any errors of fact or lapses in judgment. It will have served its purpose if it encourages readers to return to the original writings of this eminent Victorian. If he is not the 'Greatest Victorian', he is the Victorian with whom you would most want to have dinner.

A dedication is inappropriate in a book of this character. I have benefited from conversations with many friends, admirers of Bagehot, but I would like to single out Geoffrey Shaw, an American man of letters, for his belief in these memoirs and his thoughtful commentary on them.

FRANK PROCHASKA
Oxford, 2013

8 Queen's Gate Place

My dear Hutton,

I have had my share of ailments since our student days, but I saw my physician some weeks ago and the result of the examination was disquieting. As you know, I have led an active life, but as the good doctor intimated, my frail constitution, never robust, is ill suited to the strains which I place upon it. My constant movements to and from London, my rather reckless love of riding, and the exertions of editing The Economist have led to my near collapse. From all sides, I am advised to live a life of greater repose, which is difficult for a man with many commitments and ill-disguised ambition. Increasingly, I have taken to dictating from my sofa, but having to give up hunting has been dispiriting. Like the phantom in Arnold's 'Growing Old', I watch my strength decay, my pleasures fade, and 'feel the fulness of the past'.

I am not so feeble as to give way to anxious imaginings; but I would deceive myself with hopes of longevity. Like the ancient philosopher looking at the absolute, I now see the contours of my death. Consequently, I have set aside some time to reminisce about my literary and public life, what might be called the meditations of a valetudinarian in dialogue with his memories. I do not know how far these musings will take me, as this is in the hands of the gods, who do not smile on the pride of memoirists. Unhappily, the men who have tried to write their memoirs and failed are as numerous as those who have tried to be poets and failed. Reputation is a healthy and proper object of desire, but it has never been my strongest temptation.

My excuse for writing is not unlike Gibbon's, who said of his autobiography: 'My own amusement is my motive, and will be my reward.' With your kind indulgence I would like to leave these memoirs in your care. They should be hidden from the public until the author has been removed from the reach of censure.

YOURS EVER,

Walter Bagehot

CHAPTER I

A Somerset Childhood

Few things are more likely than that a man of promise will fail to live up to it, and few things more saddening than reading the memoirs of a failure. The world is full of people who have a superfluity of knowledge, culture and taste—in short all the tools of achievement—but are deficient in the latent impulse and energy which alone can turn such instruments to account. The touching remains of the young in our graveyards gives us no clue to the future fate of those persons had they survived. We can only tell a man of genius by his having produced some work of genius—nothing is so transitory as second-class fame. To writers, particularly the young, it seems that the cruel world of critics is not readily appeased; for it makes the distinction between promise and performance, and sees that juvenile triumphs are ephemeral and differ from mature accomplishment as much as bills of exchange differ from cash. If my own performance is in credit, it comes from a marshalling of energy and subscribing to the resolution: 'it's dogged as does it'.

Unlike the personages I have written about over the years, my own life has been as a gadfly, an engaged spectator—without political power, military triumphs or artistic success—connected to the well connected and to our nation's institutions. I could little have imagined how charmed my life would be when I was a breezy boy in the church and chapel fold of Langport, an old-fashioned market town in the middle of Somerset on the little river Parrett. The town's name stands for *Llan*—church, and *Porth*—harbour. To me, born in Bank House on 3 February 1826, the place was at once peaceful and bustling, a shelter and centre of the universe; but it was, and remains, little more than a village. Restricted by the flooding river, it is submissive to geography; but it has profound associations for me as a place of historic interest and natural beauty, which have been the wellspring of my vocation as a writer. My English nature is sensitive to a certain kind of scenery, and the warm colouring and gentle contour of the Somerset landscape have had a secret effect upon my nervous system and have played a part in shaping my taste and style.

My father fired my boyish imagination on telling me that one of our distant relatives was Sir Thomas Baghott, Master of the Buckhounds to James I, who fought for King Charles at Newbury. My love of the Cavalier—I associate the name with insouciance and youth—stemmed from that moment. The family name may be traced back to the Norman Conquest, where it appears in the Battle Abbey Rolls. Before the Civil War the Baghotts were owners of Prestbury and estates in Gloucestershire. My more recent forebears have been a mix of Royalist and Puritan, of the middling and upper-middling sort, merchants, bankers and ship owners, people little known to recorded history but a source of England's commercial success. Robert Bagehot, my grandfather, was a merchant who made his living shipping goods up the Parrett and selling them throughout the county under the name of the Somerset Trading Company. In 1824, his youngest child Thomas, my father, married my mother, Edith Stuckey, the niece of Samuel Stuckey, the founder of Stuckey's Banking Company.

My father, now in his eighties, is a Unitarian of methodical habits, fixed principles and kindly disposition, who had high ambitions for his only surviving son. A reserved man with the charm of modesty, he has an indifference to outward forms and a gift for resisting the temptations of cosmopolitan society; Langport is his home and he has been loath to leave it. He insisted on giving me a thorough education, having been deprived of one himself by family obligations. There was a world 'beyond his ken' he once wrote to me, a world of knowledge and usefulness that would bring me more happiness than he had found in a lifetime in business. He had a little black case, in which he kept a record of my birth and baptismal records, my school reports and university awards. To my public embarrassment but private delight, he would occasionally pull these documents from his desk and show them to family and friends, saying I was his 'greatest treasure'.

My mother, who died some years ago, was, as all who knew her will attest, a remarkable woman, with an infectious humour and intellectual vivacity that infused life into those around her. Before marrying my father, she had been married to Dr Joseph Estlin, the son of the eminent Unitarian divine John Prior Estlin of Bristol. In that city she had enjoyed a literary and intellectual culture rather wanting among bankers. Widowed at twenty-eight, she had three children by her first marriage; the first was feeble minded; the second died in a coach crash; the third succumbed to a mysterious childhood malady. She never fully recovered from these heart-breaking events. Marriage to my father brought ease and enjoyment, but also further tragedy, for their first child, my elder brother Watson, died when I was an infant.

Such terrible losses unhinged my mother's mind, leaving her in and out of sanity for much of her life. The frightening realities of her condition, which I watched with growing apprehension, would have darkened the future and scattered the hopes of many children; it would have played a more distressing part in my upbringing had it not been for my mother's resilience and my father's solicitude. Along with my father I played the part of consoler, attending to her periodic attacks of madness and melancholy. The family turned in on itself as a form of protection, and thus my life as a child was further isolated. I was hesitant to discuss my mother's condition for fear of causing embarrassment; with few friends, I was largely dependent on a supporting cast of relatives for companionship, including my half-brother Vincent, who, like my mother, needed care and attention.

It was through my mother, by turns gay and distraught, that I became sensitive to literature, especially poetry. Like Shelley's 'wretched men, cradled into poetry by wrong', she learned in suffering what she taught 'in song'. I was a son of the counting house, not the squirearchy or the manse, and she provided a literary counterpoint to the milieu of the Stuckey Bank. My childhood was a give-and-take of contrasting worlds, of poetry and commerce, art and trade, town and countryside. The underlying tension between my mother's ebullient instability and my father's conformity to the norms of business was a feature of our family life. There was even a gentle chafing in our religious observance, for my mother's dreamy Anglicanism rubbed against my father's austere Nonconformity. Each Sunday morning, I attended services conducted by my father at home and in the afternoon attended Church of England services with my mother in Langport or Huish Episcopi.

What an impoverished life it must be without a vigorous family to relieve the monotony of daily routine. I did not suffer 'The Sorrows of Young Werther'; but as a boy I travelled to and fro between the differing worlds of my parents, between the lowlands of Nonconformity and commercial Somerset and the highlands of Anglicanism and the Lakeland poets. From my father, who assembled a fine library and read the *Edinburgh* and the *Quarterly*, I gained an interest in history and politics. Guided by my mother, whose mind was touched by genius, I came under the sway of Wordsworth, whose works are the Scriptures of the intellectual life.

Like harmony in music; there is a dark
Inscrutable workmanship that reconciles
Discordant elements, makes them cling together
In one society.

In the way of children, I imperceptibly blended the contrasting characters of my parents into a hybrid sensibility.

When I was a child, the family moved from Bank House to Herd's Hill, an unpretentious country house with a fine garden, which had been built by my Bagehot grandparents. There I received an education and found the support that gave me the cheerfulness that became a feature of my early life. I never had to endure the humiliation of youth, but explored at will under the shelter of a privileged childhood. It was privileged in ways other than money and status, for I lived in beautiful surroundings and roamed in the open air, a world removed from the crippling intensity of Mill's education or the loveless childhood of Lord Shaftesbury. In contrast, my home life was loving and lenient, which little inhibited my unregenerate devotion to danger and play. My robust humour was in the same key as my mother's, which was somewhat out of tune with my father's. From her I inherited an infectious enjoying instinct lacking in dissent, and from him a love of the past, which are the twin pillars of conservatism.

Although my father is a Liberal in politics, he has conservative leanings typical of his profession, which the harrowing history of his generation heightened. My parents and grandparents grew up with the French Revolution and the wars with France, which made a powerful impression on them. That world is now so far removed from us that we cannot comprehend its ever having existed; but in those days, grown-up people talked of nothing but French perfidy; even in deepest Somerset, dispossessed refugees from Paris appeared from time to time with their lurid tales of republican barbarism. If my family believed all they heard of French savagery and threats of invasion, they must have been tormented indeed. Whatever their social background, the English could see that the Revolution had deteriorated into terror, irreligion, regicide, and a military dictatorship that threatened the nations of Europe. Whenever radicals called for domestic reform, the cry was heard: 'What, you want a REVOLUTION, do you?' followed by a recital of French extremism.

The French Revolution terrified mankind all through the period which Dr Arnold called 'the misused trial-time of modern Europe'. The reaction to Gallic principles had mischievous effects. Nothing is so cruel as fear, and it infused into the minds of the English a spirit of reaction. The vast majority of the English people were determined to put down French principles, which included what we should all now consider obvious improvements and rational reforms. A generation in England was so frightened by the Reign of Terror that they thought it could only be prevented by another Reign of Terror at home, which led to draconian laws and an unfeeling obtuseness. The vice of the authorities and the public in those years was a propensity to an exaggerated opposition inherent in human nature and a forgetfulness of the pain that their own acts produced—a habit which adhered to official rules and established maxims, and which refused to be shocked by the evident human suffering. The result of this habit was the excitement of the habit precisely opposed to it.

Children are good listeners and my generation inherited many of the anti-Gallic opinions of their parents and grandparents. The phrase 'Boney will get you', spoken only half in jest, was still heard in English homes to stifle disobedience. As a headstrong and solitary child, I lived a life of wayward impulse in a family who excused my youthful prejudices and exuberant behaviour.

Oh what a wilderness were this sad world
If man were always man, and never child.

In a letter to Horace Walpole, Thomas Gray said that even great
statesmen were once 'dirty boys playing at cricket'. For my part,
I feel older, but not much wiser than when I was but a dirty boy
playing in the garden of Herd's Hill, or climbing the rocks on our
seaside holidays in Devon. While I enjoyed riding and rambling
in the open as much as the next boy, I cut a poor figure at games,
preferring to amuse myself with ends of verse, the sayings of
philosophers, and the vicissitudes of history.

I recently discovered some letters of mine to and from my
parents in a chest in Herd's Hill. In one of them dated 17 June
1833, my father wrote: 'Mamma tells me you are becoming a poet
and I shall look forward some day or other to our having a "Sir
Walter" in our own family. Your sword is sent, and tomorrow is
the anniversary of the battle of Waterloo, I suppose you will be
very grand on the occasion. How would you have liked living at
Brussels when the cannons began to roar and the soldiers were
summoned to the field?' Mercifully, my poetic effusions are now
lost, but I recall the sword given to me at the age of seven by my
father. In my beaming imagination, it served as a weapon against
the French, in which the rose hips in our garden played their
sacrificial part. All children have a world of their own, as distinct
from that of the grown-up people who orbit around them. About
this interior existence children are dumb, but I hacked at the
infelicitous bushes until I did not altogether reject the idea that
our garden was the battleground of Waterloo and I the most
adventurous of English officers.

Although history and poetry were mainstays of my reading,
I relished the religious writing for children in the 1830s. My
father's evangelical sister, Aunt Reynolds, gave me a copy of *Daily
Food for Christians*, which I wore out with reading. In childhood

I uttered the words, but it was only later when I became half unwilling to utter them, that they began to have a meaning. Children have the impulse to believe but little which can be called a religion; the shows of this world, the play of its lights and shadows, suffice. It is in the collision of our nature, which occurs in youth, that the first real sensation of faith is felt. Conscience is often then morbidly acute; a flush passes over the youthful mind; the guiding instinct is keen and strong, like the passions with which it contends. Our religion commences at the first struggle of our nature.

Little did I suspect as a boy that my Christian education was influenced by the religious revival which the apostasy of the French had aroused decades earlier. Jacobinism kindled English piety, and the mixing together of politics and faith had long-lasting effects. In my childhood, Hannah More's anti-Jacobin *Tracts*, written in her Wrington retreat in the Mendip Hills, could still be found in the homes of the Somerset poor, a rebuke to radicals like Paine and his Chartist descendants. In the counter-revolutionary decades, evangelicals and conservatives were quick to link indecency and radicalism, savagery and unbelief, and draped themselves in piety and respectability. Respectability is piety made secular; along with its attendant seriousness, it continues to shape the manners and morals of England, with varied results for our institutions and culture.

Benevolence and moral reformation were ubiquitous features of the religious revival of the early decades of this century. In an era of counter-revolution and social disorder, people of all sects and classes raised good works to a new status. A religion which did not combine its subjective faith with a strenuous labour for the good of others was hardly held to possess any principle worth proclaiming. 'We are now overrun with philanthropy, and God knows where it will stop, or whither it will lead us,' wrote Greville in his *Journal*. The courtesans and painted ladies of

Stuart England have vanished, replaced by lady bountifuls and Mrs Pardiggles who busy themselves setting out stalls for benighted heathens and the deserving poor. When Dickens acquaints us with the wives and daughters of clerks and tradesmen getting up some dingy mission room for charitable purposes, one may wonder where such enthusiasm will lead.

I admire my family for its many local kindnesses—my mother and her brother, 'Uncle Stuckey', were noted for their Christian charity in Langport and the country round. But one may have a melancholy doubt whether philanthropy generally does more harm than good. Philanthropy does great good, but it also augments so much vice, multiplies so much suffering, and brings to life great populations to suffer, that it is open to argument whether it be or be not an evil to the world. And this is entirely because excellent people fancy that they can do much by rapid action—that they will most benefit the world when they most relieve their own feelings; that as soon as an evil is seen 'something' ought to be done to stay and prevent it. One may incline to hope that the balance of good and evil favours benevolence, but its burden of harm might have been spared us if our philanthropists and religious enthusiasts had not inherited a passion for instant action and took the trouble to think.

In my youth, the melancholy roar of unbelief was as yet faint, for the disinterested mind, disengaged from party or sect, had only begun to operate over the whole range of human circumstance with scientific precision. In Somerset, religion was enveloping, doubt exceptional; the idea of a knowable, Godless world made little sense to an anti-intellectual people still largely dependent on the land and the rhythm of the seasons. The Christian virtues of hard work, self-help and mutual support were obligatory. The religious sects, each with an array of free associations, provided the wherewithal of well-being in a little-administered world. Most children received scant instruction other than that provided by the charity and Sunday schools, which filled their minds with the fear of God and the necessity of industrious labour.

The recent educational reforms, which are now shifting the balance of education to the state, have something to recommend them, but the limits placed on religious instruction are damaging to our ancient Christian culture. It is one thing to have a dogmatic religion implanted in children from their baby-hood, however less dogmatic their views may become as they grow to be men and women, and quite another to bring up children without any religious creed at all. We have yet to see what a nation would be like whose men and women had never had any religious training whatever given to them as children. Christianity has always been more than a source of discipline; it is a fount of social authority and a treasury of consolations. If it surrenders its responsibility as an instrument of moral education, from where will moral training come?

In my childhood, farmers, artisans and tradesmen made up most of the parishioners in Langport; some of them had never been to Taunton, much less to London or to Leeds. In outlook and traditions they had little in common with the blackened proletariat of the northern industrial cities. They were Church and King people, settled in their habits, chary of change, hostile to London officialdom and wary of outsiders. Many of them looked upon a Chartist demonstration as they would a foreign invasion. Their close contact with the natural world shaped their minds and imaginations and instilled in them a natural conservatism; deference, underpinned by a foundation of religious instruction, steadied the social fabric. In the genial and lazy counties the inhabitants would say that Queen Victoria ruled by right of birth and the grace of God. To comprehend what England was like only a decade ago, you should fancy a set of Dorsetshire peasants assembled by the mud-pond of the village solemnly answering questions about the complexities of suffrage reform. The utmost stretch of wisdom the conclave could arrive at would be: 'Ah, sir, you gentlefolks do know; and the Queen, God bless her, will see us righted.'

The Langport of my youth was a community of gradations— of birth and rank, land and trade, education and religion. My weekly appearance at church with my mother, in which she was treated with cordial respect by all and sundry, was part of my social awakening. So too was seeing the regard shown to my father and my uncle at the Bank. Being the child of a prominent Somerset family invigorated my sense of the importance of deference and hierarchy in the making of civility and social stability, refinement and personal aspiration. The English, as Lord Palmerston declared, are a cheerful people, who live under a constitution in which individuals aspire to raise themselves in the social order not through violence and illegality but through talent, energy and persevering good conduct. The principle of equality, which socialists and Americans extol with doctrinaire fervour, not only lacks charm but is fatal to that development of individual originality and greatness by which the past progress of the human race has been achieved, and from which all future progress is to be anticipated.

There is no method by which men can be both free and equal. If it be said that people are all alike, that the world is a plain with no natural valleys and no natural hills, the picturesqueness of existence is destroyed, and, what is worse, the instinctive emulation by which the dweller in the valley is stimulated to climb the hill is annihilated and becomes impossible. In contrast to our system of *removable inequalities*, there is an opposite system which prevails in the East—the system of *irremovable inequalities*, of hedged-in castes, which no one can enter but by birth, and from which no born member can issue forth. In England, this system needs no attack, for it has no defenders. Everyone is ready to admit that it cramps originality, by defining our work irrespective of our qualities and before we were born; that it retards progress, by restraining the wholesome competition between class and class, and the wholesome migration from class to class, which are the best and strongest instruments of social improvement.

≈≈◎≈≈

The years following the great Congress of Vienna were a time of sullenness and difficulty in England. We had vanquished Napoleon, but we had no pleasure in what came after him. Our victory had been great, but it had no fruits. The cause which agitated us was gone; there was no longer a noise of victories in the air; continental affairs were dead and despotic. We scarcely liked to think that we had made them so; with weary dissatisfaction we turned to our own condition. This was profoundly unsatisfactory. There was an incessant distress running through society. Trade was depressed, agriculture ruinous, the working classes singularly disaffected by closed mills and scanty employment. In the straitened years after the defeat of Napoleon the records are full of Hampden Clubs, 'Spencean Philanthropists' and other radical associations, all desiring the reform of politics and the social economy. Meanwhile, the stagnated political system estranged the growing middle class, which felt powerless in the face of the timorous immobility of the aristocracy. Taxation was oppressive, public expenditure lavish. The King, an overgrown voluptuary, lived beyond his means. The existence of slavery in our colonies offended the principles of Christianity and the natural sentiments of simple men. The nation's decayed institutions called out for reform.

And so it happened that my childhood coincided with an era of remarkable political progress, which resolved many of the tensions and troubles that had built up in the debilitating decades of reaction to French principles and French arms. In the late 1820s, a new generation came to influence public affairs, reformers who did not remember the horrors of the French Revolution and Napoleon and who had been bored to tears hearing their parents talk about them. In 1828, when I was still an infant, Lord John Russell introduced a bill to repeal the Test and Corporation Acts, which had excluded Dissenters from office. Its passage was a cause of great celebration in the Unitarian circles of my father. Four years later, as I sat poring over the works of Wordsworth and Sir Walter Scott with my mother, I remember my father and his Whig friends discussing the merits of the Reform Bill, which was then going through Parliament. It marked my political awakening.

To reformers, the French Revolution of 1830 broke with magical power. Even to soberer persons this new revolution seemed to prove that change, even great change, was not so mischievous as had been said—that the good of 1789 might be gained without the evil, and that it was absurd not to try reform when the unreformed world contained so much which was miserable and difficult to bear. The Reform Bill of 1832 fulfilled the dreams of young reformers,

> The meagre, stale, forbidding ways
> Of custom, law, and statute, took at once
> The attraction of a country in romance!

And there came upon them eager thoughts that they might still be

> called upon to exercise their skill,
> Not in Utopia, subterranean fields,
> Or some secreted island, Heaven knows where!
> But in the very world, which is the world
> Of all of us . . .

'Althorp carried the Bill' was the ecstatic cry in our household when the great Reform Act of 1832 altered the ever-varying Constitution of England. The romance of the measure has since died away and in our sober history the men who passed it—Lords Althorp, Grey and Russell—are now seldom mentioned; but in that generation it was like a little revolution—which really changed so much, and which seemed to change so much more. But what was this great 'Bill', which it was such an achievement to pass? It was not one of which the political world itself strongly approved. If left to itself that world would have rejected it, for it affected many private interests. It changed the franchise of every constituency, and therefore the seat of every member; it abolished the seats of many, and eliminated the right of nomination to seats possessed by others. Few things are more repugnant to a politician than the abolition of his office, but in 1832 some very good men did some very good work in abolishing themselves.

In the end, the Reform Act destroyed many old things and altered many others, not least a variety of rights of suffrage. The differing franchises of the unreformed Parliament grew as all English things grow—by day-by-day alterations from small beginnings. Ultimately, this led to great confusion. Nothing could be more certain than that a system constructed in this manner must sooner or later need great alteration. The public was asked to be content not only with old clothes, but with much-patched old clothes, which they were denied the power to patch again. And this, sooner or later, they were sure to refuse. By 1832, there was a grave necessity of changing it. The longer the system went on without change, the more certain it was to need change. Some new class was sure in course of time to grow up for which the fixed system provided no adequate representatives.

In 1832, such a class had arisen of the first magnitude. The trading wealth of the country had created a new world which had no voice in Parliament. The power of the richest peers and squires was much too great when compared with their share in the life of the nation, just as that of the trading class was too weak. Some of the greatest towns, Birmingham and Manchester, were left without any members at all, but in most other towns the best of the middle class felt that they had no adequate power. The Reform Bill amended all this. It gave members to large towns and cities, and changed the franchise, so that in all boroughs the middle classes obtained predominant power. And no one can deny that the good so done was immense; indeed, no one does now deny it, for the generation of Tories that did so has passed away.

For all its merits, the Act did not produce of itself the new heaven and earth that its more ardent supporters expected of it. It did nothing to remove the worst evils from which the country suffered, for those evils were not political but economic. The doctrine of protection then reigned over all the nation, and while it did so no real cure for those evils was possible. But the Act, coming as it did when a new generation was prepared to make use of it, got rid entirely of the 'cruel spirit' by which our distressed had been previously repressed, and which was as great an evil as those distresses themselves. It introduced many improvements—municipal reform and tithe reform among them—in which the business-like habit of mind due to the greater power of the working classes mainly helped and diffused a sweeter and better spirit through society.

But these benefits exacted a price, though its payment was long deferred. The reformers of 1832 dealt with the evils of their time in an English way, without much thinking of anything else. And exactly in that English way, they discarded some of the more valuable parts of the unreformed political machine that had grown up without design. They made a grievous mistake in destroying the variety in the old system of representation. They raised the standard household franchise in some boroughs and lowered it in others, and in this way they changed the cardinal principle of the system which they inherited, for uniformity became the rule instead of variety. All this worked well enough at first, but in our time we have seen the harm of it. In a few years there may be only one sort of vote and only one size of constituency all over England and then the reign of monotony will be complete. Once you establish any uniform franchise short of universal suffrage, then it at once becomes a question, what sort of franchise is it to be? Those under it will say that they are most unjustly excluded, and they will raise the familiar cry—the cry of class legislation.

***

Such issues have preoccupied me of late, but they were far from my mind on hearing the animated discussions of the Reform Bill as a boy. Under my governess, Miss Jones, I was not reading Hansard but learning the rudiments of Latin. At the age of eight, I moved on to Langport Grammar School as a day scholar, where the formidable schoolmaster, Mr Quekett, encouraged my love of maths and poetry, subjects which reflected the contrasting interests of my father and mother. I took unusual pleasure from a mix of solitude and monotonous study, which is the legitimate food of a self-relying nature. At home, I enjoyed informal reading in the family library. Some people say there was a time when there was no book they could not enjoy. In childhood there is a presumption that the obvious thing to do with a horse is to ride it; with a cake to eat it; and with a sixpence to spend it. I took this further and thought the natural thing to do with a book was to read it. Indeed, there is an argument from design in the action: what was the purpose of a book if not to be read? In childhood, you no more think of the consequence of deriving knowledge from reading than you expect a prize for spinning a top. Without forethought or expectation, you spin the top and read the book; and out of it you develop a sense of the unity and plenitude of the world.

At thirteen I began my studies at Bristol College. My mother would have preferred me to go to Westminster or Harrow, but I deferred to my father's wishes and my own desire to be close to home. The school, unlike many schools of the day, gave emphasis to science; Anglican services were optional. The teaching was of a high order, with lectures on natural philosophy by the physiologist William Carpenter, and on the origins of civilisation by Dr James Prichard, who was related to my mother by her first marriage. My own course consisted of classics, German, Hebrew and mathematics, but I learned much else through conversations and private reading. In spite of the rather antagonistic influence of the able, scientific men from whom I learned so much, I came under the spell of Kant, whose distinction between the accessible world of the senses and the world accessible to the moral faculties I found persuasive.

Much of the time at Bristol I was on my own and was sometimes taught in a class by myself. The most stimulating solitude is solitude in the midst of society, and that is what my schooling provided. I was an indulged child, and my academic leanings combined with awkwardness in relating to my own age group. Pupils are divided into scholars and hearties; given my studious nature and dislike of school games, I was in the former camp, surrounded, but for a few friends, by boys who equated bookishness with priggishness. I managed to get steadily to work, which was a comfort, and made me much less dismal than I might otherwise have been, being away from my parents. To my delight, I occasionally dined with Dr Prichard at Red Lodge in Clifton. The habits and tastes that pervaded the house were salutary, while the knowledge which I gleaned from Dr Prichard and his learned circle nourished my own channels of thought.

My education was a mix of loose and unplanned reading, which benefited from a more rigorous kind, which was imposed on me from without. The terrible difficulty of early life is that pastors and masters compel boys to a distinct mastery of that which they do not wish to learn. Decorum is the essence, pomposity the advantage, of tutors. There is nothing to be said for a teacher who is not dry, and I look back with gratitude on the masters who drummed into me the rudiments of learning. Carlyle describes with bitter satire the fate of one of his heroes who was obliged to acquire whole systems of information in which he, the hero, saw no use. And this is the very point—dry language, tedious mathematics, a thumbed grammar form gradually an interior separate intellect, exact in its information, rigid in its requirements, disciplined in its exercises. The early natural fancy touching the far extremities of the universe, lightly playing with the scheme of all things, grows together with the precise, compacted memory slowly accumulating special facts, exact habits, clear and painful conceptions. At last the clouds sweep away; we find that these exercises which puzzled us, these languages which we hated, these details which we despised, are the instruments of true thought, are the very keys and openings, the exclusive access to the knowledge which we loved.

Every child believes what he is told, and probably everyone's memory will carry him back to the horrid mass of miscellaneous confusion which he acquired by believing all he heard. Education should beat out of our minds groundless prejudice and credulous expectation. Its use is to make a good *learner*. Instruction is to the mind what the telescope is to the eye. To an uncultivated intellect what is distant will always be invisible, but a well-trained mind is habitually able to look into the future. But although the public education of the average Englishman has merits—it is fit for training ordinary men—it tends to diminish self-confidence. It teaches boys that they are no better than other boys, and the world a medley in which it is difficult to conquer and impossible to rule.

'At sixteen,' says Mr Disraeli, 'everyone believes he is the most peculiar man who ever lived.' The difficulty is to retain this proud belief, not only to have lofty ambitions but to hold to them in the face of the facts of growing up. As a boy, the world does not believe in you. You fancy you have a call to a great career, but no one else imagines that you even fancy it. For fear of ridicule you dare not say it out loud. Meanwhile, the illusions of youth pass away, and with them goes all intellectual courage. Most children have scarcely the wish to form their own creed, to think for themselves, to act upon their own beliefs; they try to be sensible and end up being dull; they fear to be eccentric and end by being commonplace. I was preserved from the characteristic degradation of well-intentioned and erudite youth by two great counteracting influences—an enlivening sense of humour and a genuine interest in great issues.

> What are numbers knit
> By force or custom? Man who man would be,
> Must rule the empire of himself.

⚜

As a boy I became an avid reader of history. It is said that history is not a fit subject for the young, that the reading of great books should be left to adults and will only perplex children with conflicting facts remote from their experience. The reply is that although children cannot thoroughly understand complex events there is a good deal that can only be truly apprehended for the first time while young. Small sciences are the labours of manhood. Youth enjoys a principle of consolidation. It begins with the whole, the round universe being the plaything of the child. The young mind shoots out vaguely and crudely into the unknown. There are no boundaries to its wandering vision. We begin with the infinite and eternal, which shall never be understood; and these form a framework, a set of coordinates to which we refer all that we later learn. Like the Greek, 'we look up to the whole sky, and are lost in the one and the all'. In the end we classify and enumerate, study each star, calculate distances, and find precision in the everlasting. So too with history. Somehow the whole comes in childhood, the details in adulthood. Not today or yesterday, but long ago, in the first dawn of reason, we find guidance in the flow of fancy. What we learn later is but the accurate littleness of the great topic.

The whole of history gradually came into focus in my education; the astonishing story going far back to the times of the patriarchs: the observant Greeks, the stately Romans, the watching Jews, the uncouth Goths, the ghastly Huns, the settled picture of the static East, the advance of the restless West, the rise and fall of the cold and classical civilizations, the rough impetuous Middle Ages, until we reach the warm picture of England's greatness, ourselves and home. For a child, all roads lead to home. When past events are linked to one's own place or family they stay in the memory; they set one apart and give romance and dimension to one's sense of self. My own understanding of history was taking shape, my mind suggestible.

Local legends and events gave immediacy to my reading. 'We love the play-place of our early days,' wrote Cowper. It was from the summit of Herd's Hill, where I roamed as a boy, that Richard Baxter as Chaplain to the Cromwellian Army viewed with Fairfax the flight of the Royalist Army under Lord Goring after the battle of Langport. A little further west from Herd's Hill along the meandering Parrett is Burrow Mump, from Norman times a site of military interest and a place of haunting beauty. In my childhood, a Georgian church stood on its brow, replacing the medieval church of St Michael, which once formed a sanctuary for Royalist troops during the Civil War. Over the years it has become a deserted ruin, a monument to the picturesque, a symbol of impermanence and waning faith.

The legend-filled landscape of Somerset and the riches of the family library gave shape to my disposition; it is that of the historian, which is the tendency that inclines men to take an interest in actions rather than objects. Some people are born scientific, interested largely in nature. They are curious about snails and butterflies, delighted at an ichthyosaurus and excited at a polyp. They attain renown in studying pebbles. In the highest cases they know the great causes of grand phenomena; their minds are directed not to the actions of man but to the scenery in which man lives; not to the inhabitants of this world but to the world itself. What compels men to take an interest in what they do take an interest in is perhaps insoluble; but in the case of scientists it would seem to result from the absence of an intense and vivid nature. The inclination that draws attention from that in which it can feel sympathy to that in which it cannot, seems to arise from a want of sympathy. The tendency to study trees and stones rather than men and women suggests a scientific aloofness, which casts a chill on human glory.

The disposition of most people is the opposite of scientific. The world has a vested interest in itself, and the tendency of man is to take an interest in man. The wingspan of finches and the size of the planets fill only the remote corners of the brain for most of us; the greater part of our faculties is expended on man and his fellows. Indeed, this is not simply an intellectual contemplation; we not only observe, but act. The impulse to busy ourselves with the affairs of men goes further than the simple attempt to know and comprehend. It warms us with a further life; it incites us to stir and influence affairs; its animated energy will not rest till it has hurried us into toil and conflict. If the scientific mind is one of calm, the minds of most of us are distinguished by restlessness and agitation. At this stage, historians, who instinctively select human action for occupation and scrutiny, draw back. They may indulge in eager admiration or lasting hatred, but to analyse and to know is typically sufficient for them; they can bear detachment.

'Why', it is often asked, 'is history dull? It is the narrative of life, and life is of all things the most interesting.' The answer is plain: it is written by men who are dull, who take too little interest in life, in whom sluggishness predominates over passion and for whom the study is a refuge from the world. The impassive Gibbon placidly contemplated the conflicts of his day and watched a revolution from the reporters' gallery. Such chill aloofness of temper and insensibility to impulse gives an idea of the historian as he is likely to be. Disengagement and consequent dullness seem to be features of the historical disposition. If my own disposition is that of the historian, it is not without impulse and ardour. Since I was a young man, I have been fascinated by politics, parliaments and the affairs of men, in which, over the years, I have become an active participant and reporter, albeit calmed by a measure of ironic distance. I am an historian *manqué*.

꙰

CHAPTER II

A London Education

O N leaving Bristol College, I had quiet thoughts of attending
Oxford, which would have pleased my mother; but my
father disliked the aristocratic leanings of the University and
objected to the doctrinal tests which were then required.
Notwithstanding that Oxford exacted assent to the Thirty-Nine
Articles, few Oxford-bred men could give any rational account
of them, or the weary controversies out of which their nomenclature arose. The English nation has no opinion of them at all;
since our fathers fell asleep there has been no bona fide discussion
of them. My own faith was more in keeping with my mother's
Anglicanism than my father's Nonconformity. Indeed, I have
never been a Unitarian. Had I gone to Oxford and been asked to
sign the Thirty-Nine Articles I would have said, 'yes, if you give
me a pen'. The ancient University would have been agreeable to
me for its illustrious history, the beauty of its meadows and cloisters, and the opportunity to measure my wits against some of the
finest minds of my generation.

But Oxford in the 1840s, though undergoing modest reform,
was not intellectually demanding; its education operated as a
narcotic rather than as a stimulant. It trained a large number of

men, but most of them were more interested in winning prizes than in finding truth. Apart from the generation of eager-minded men, of whom Newman, Whately and Arnold were the best known, Oxford exerted little influence on the mind of England. Most of its students devoted themselves to a single profession and were overtaken by a kind of sacred torpidity. Oxford, it has been said, 'disheartens a man early'. It serves as a 'graduating machine', with the colleges—monopolist residences—hotels without bells. The roads out of it lead to the colonies or the parish; a fellowship may be likened to a long walk with a church at the end of it. The most characteristic of Oxford men labour quietly, delicately, and sometimes usefully, in a confined sphere; they wish for nothing more. Apathy, indifference and a sleepy intellect are the cultural norm, in which, as one of Emerson's stories says of the place, 'there is nothing true and nothing new, —and no matter'.

At the age of sixteen, I began my studies at University College London, which did not impose doctrinal tests. It was an institution full of the high ambition of its founders, whose exacting standards were akin to those of the men who founded Bristol College. If a student did not succeed, it was not from a want of institutional aspiration, but from idleness, folly, or the distractions of the capital. To ensure that I did not chance the dangers and temptations of London, my parents insisted that I treat my Aunt and Uncle Reynolds, who lived in Hampstead, as a second home. My first residence was that of Professor John Hoppus, a Nonconformist, who had a house suitable for students in Camden Town, where my father and I presented ourselves in October 1842. In writing to my mother shortly after my arrival, I noted the palpable contrast with the beauties of Somerset and admitted feeling rather homesick. I missed the open air and the evenings at home, although I managed by dint of hard work to take some pleasure from London, despite the sounds and smells, dust and smoke.

Cultivated dawdling often does duty for work in polished academical circles, but the curriculum at University College demanded more. My studies required a rapid acquisition of knowledge on a host of subjects: logic, Latin and Greek, mathematics and chemistry, moral philosophy and political economy. Augustus De Morgan lectured on mathematics and philosophy, and Henry Malden and George Long on Greek. Professor Morgan had one eye and a large white face. He spoke very well and seemed interested in mathematics as if he were lecturing on it for the first time, and had not been going over the same ground for ten years. I admired Mr Malden, who gave us an immense quantity of information on all manner of subjects. He had been a moderately pleasant-looking man before he had the smallpox, which made him the most pitiful creature man had ever seen. He dressed in clothes which looked as if moths had long been their familiar inhabitants. Professor Long was a withered-looking man, sceptical and suspicious, but very clear-headed, with rather a narrow disciplinarian mind and a dry humour. He was always quoting Aristotle as the greatest thinker who ever lived, a view which I dismissed at the time but am now disposed to entertain.

Intense effort, punctuated by bouts of ill health and self-doubt, marked my years at University College. Classics and mathematics took up much of my time, while poetry and prose provided intellectual enjoyment and nourished feeling as well as mind. Literature should be the delight of life, but delight seeks companionship.

Surprised by joy, impatient as the Wind—
I turned to share the transport—Oh! with whom . . . ?

I was fortunate in finding good companions in Richard Hutton, William Roscoe and a distant cousin Timothy Smith Osler, who shared my pleasure in debate and ideas. In youth, the real plastic energy is not in tutors or lectures or in books 'got up', but in Wordsworth and Shelley, in the writings everyone reads and everyone admires. In the argumentative walk or disputatious lounge—fresh thought on fresh thought—in mirth and refutation—in ridicule and laughter—one enjoys the free play of the mind, which is rarely found outside a college. Gower Street and the dreary chain of squares from Euston to Bloomsbury were for us the scenes of discussions as eager and as abstract as ever took place in the sedate cloisters of Oxford or Cambridge. Hutton well remembers a spirited argument as to whether the so-called logical principle of identity (A is A) was entitled to rank as a 'law of thought' or was only a postulate of language. As a result we wandered up and down Regent Street for hours in the vain attempt to find Oxford Street.

Though I held my own on the London pavements—my friends accused me of intellectual arrogance—I had less confidence in the examination rooms and suffered periods of acute anxiety about my abilities. Distrustful of my powers of endurance and dreaming of failure, the day before my exams in 1843 I collapsed with a cough and breathlessness, which I attributed to consumption inherited from my mother's family. Despite my croakings and forebodings—my headaches and giddiness—my fears growing faster than my hopes—I passed in the first class in classical honours. On the heels of this success, my ailments became a worry to my parents; at the end of my exams it was decided that I should return home until the New Year, thus missing the autumn term. My consolation came in the shape of a horse, a grey, which gave me much pleasure during the months I remained at Herd's Hill. I returned to University College in January 1844 refreshed.

The political atmosphere in London was protean, with agitated assemblages of competing causes, which created great, raucous scenes inside the meeting rooms. I was then working through my political beliefs and found much that was instructive, in presentation as well as statecraft. The metropolis, then as now, was a better site of political education than Oxford or Cambridge and suited my growing interest in practical politics, economical science and oratory. Hutton and I spent many an enjoyable hour listening to the orations of Cobden and Bright and compared all we heard to the peerless disquisitions of Burke and Macaulay. I still recall Bright's triumphs in Drury Lane and Covent Garden. There was a racy fun and sentiment in his speeches, which even now make them capital reading. Of all our recent politicians he may prove to be the best remembered because his orations were the most amusing.

The meetings of the Anti-Corn Law League were, side by side with the Chartist meetings of the northern operatives, an expression of the distinctive Manchester philosophy; for good and ill, both movements were potent in our national life. Nowadays, a new generation is attaining life and vigour to whom both creeds are a matter of history. Thirty years ago, they were dynamic forms of discontent and a counterpoise was wanting. While sceptical of the Chartist demands, I recall a memorable Chartist meeting addressed by Henry Vincent—he was opposed to physical force and spent half his time talking about Christian principles—and came away deeply impressed by the eloquence and cleverness of the man, who was not entirely in error as to his political views.

As the son of a banker attached to free trade, I was naturally drawn to meetings of the Anti-Corn Law League. The rhetoric was impressive, but there was a great want of argument in many of the harangues, which contained not 'one halfpenny-worth of bread to this intolerable deal of sack!' Eloquence is well and good, but in treating of great practical questions one requires well-grounded and enlarged principles. In a notable meeting at Covent Garden Theatre I heard Daniel O'Connell, who spoke for two hours in the most eloquent manner I had ever heard. It was an imposing sight to see the whole house crammed full of admirers, who rose at once upon his entrance and cheered his every utterance. I had to stand the whole evening but with no reason to complain. I was full of it for a day or two, and remember it still as if it were yesterday. Never had I such a distinct notion of the greatness of London as when I came out of the meeting and saw how little interest this great event seemed to excite among the distracted throngs in the nearby streets. It provided a political lesson of the first magnitude.

I had been reading Carlyle's *French Revolution* at the time. Political science is a hard subject, but Carlyle's rejection of all the common expedients struck me as strangely fascinating. He seemed utterly disbelieving in the usefulness of any institutions. For hereditary monarchy and hereditary aristocracy he had a thorough contempt. Representative assemblies he called National Debating Clubs, and the right of suffrage he saw as the power to send a tiny fraction of the dumb voice to the central spouting club. He was in favour of a natural aristocracy, as he called it. State power should be directed by the highest minds in every generation. There is much to be said for this opinion, but my own view was that the highest intellects should rather be engaged in communicating new truth to mankind, or labouring to illustrate known truth and to instruct the mass of the population in old and valuable knowledge. This is a far higher way of influencing the happiness of the world than the application of physical force to protect men's lives and property.

It is a not infrequent source of error to confound the influence of the finest minds over their fellow men by persuasion and conviction with the government by laws and Acts of Parliament. The two things seem very distinct to me. Dr Arnold's theory that government ought to be sovereign over human life seems grounded on nothing else but the assumption that the government by argument and the government by force must necessarily be the same. At University College we had a debate on the question 'whether government ought to interfere with the dissemination of blasphemous or seditious publications'. As a member of the debating club, I took the negative. The advocates of suppression, I reminded my listeners, would do well to consider the fact that the works of Shelley—the poet of all others upon whom the mantle of Milton appears in the last generation to have descended—could not be legally published in this country. We were not yet entitled to despise the licensers who wished to mutilate *Paradise Lost*.

In the debate, I argued that laws as laws neither convince nor persuade but threaten; they address neither the intellect nor the conscience but fear and the will. No law could promise the mental pleasures arising from the acquisition of the truth, or from the peace of a satisfied conscience. Over belief government is utterly powerless. Being unable to guide the minds of its subjects to what opinions it deems true, it must not presume to meddle with their professions. Is there anything more terrible than the situation of a government which rules without apprehension over a people of hypocrites—which is flattered by the press and cursed in the inner chambers—which prides itself on the affection and attachment of its subjects and knows not that those subjects are leagued together against it by a freemasonry of hatred? Profound and ingenious policy, not to cure the disease but to remove the only symptoms by which it can be certainly known: this is to leave the serpent his sting and take from him his warning rattle.

Government, I reasoned, should never interfere with the indecorous expression of opinions; first, because the effect of legislative interference in controversies has ever been to make an approximation to candour compulsory on one side but to encourage on the other side violence, calumny and bigotry; secondly, because many of the writings that would be suppressed by legal penalties have an important part to play in the removal of social encumbrances; thirdly, because no one knows what blasphemy is nor what sedition is, but all know that they are vague words which can be fitted to any meaning that shall please the ruling powers. I deemed it demonstrated from these considerations that all restriction was unwise and all suppression impolitic, and that all attempts to guide the expression of opinions were so many incitements to insincerity and hypocrisy. This address, delivered at the age of seventeen, I showed to my parents with adolescent pride. My father encouraged me to consider a career in the law.

⚜

Though our little circle at University College often touched on the law and politics, much of the talk was of a philosophical and religious nature. My reading centred on philosophy, poetry and theology, together with the more sharply defined science of my classes. At home, there was much discussion of my future. While my father thought a legal training desirable, my mother, concerned for my health and thinking me unsuited to the strains of academic study, wanted me to forgo the life of a mawkish scholar and return to Langport and turn my attention to commerce and the practical details of daily life. All paths were open to good sense, she wrote to me at the time, but she urged me to fully appreciate my father's cleverness in business: 'If he were to die now, which God forbid! I am sure I should at once wish you to understand *what business is.*'

By the time I completed my Bachelor of Arts degree in 1846, it was assumed that I would read for the Bar; and since the next hurdle was to become a Master of Arts, I moved to lodgings in Great Coram Street and settled down to a further two years of study. Shakespeare, Keats, Shelley and Wordsworth, Coleridge, Martineau and Newman, all in their way exerted a particular influence on me, along with those I was bound to study: the Greek philosophers, Hume, Kant and John Stuart Mill. As Leibniz said, there are 'secrets in the art of thinking as in all other arts'. My hope was to amass sufficient learning to feed the imagination and unlock the secret of originality.

My readings were an apt preparation for a highlight of my student days, the regular breakfasts with Henry Crabb Robinson, one of the original founders of University College, who had known nearly every literary man worth knowing in England and Germany for fifty years. He lived near the College and enjoyed bringing together the elder students with an interest in literature. It was a privilege to join Wordsworth's good companion, to whom the poet had dedicated his *Memorials of a Tour in Italy*. 'Old Crabb', as we called him, probably never appeared to so much advantage, or showed all the best of his nature, so well as in those parties. He liked fun and movement, and disliked the sort of dignity which shelters stupidity. But there was little to gratify the unintellectual part of man at these breakfasts. The more astute of his guests took breakfast before they came, for our host usually had forgotten to make tea, and one sat in agony as the promised delicacies were interrupted by dishes of Goethe and Schiller. I well remember bringing along the poet Arthur Clough, just down from Oxford, who sat in a kind of terror for the whole breakfast, and muttered in mute wonder as he came away, 'not at all your regular patriarch'.

Mr Robinson used to read Wordsworth to us, but I doubt whether he read the best poems, and even those he did read rather suffered from coming at a time when you wanted to laugh and not to meditate. Wordsworth was a solitary man, and it is only in solitude that his best poems, or his most characteristic poems, can be truly felt or apprehended. There are some at which I never look, even now, without thinking of the wonderful and dreary faces which Clough used to make while Mr Robinson was reading them. From time to time Mr Robinson, who *thought* me a modern youth, quarrelled with me for urging that Hazlitt was a much greater writer than Charles Lamb. It was a harmless opinion which Mr Robinson met with this outburst: 'You, sir, YOU prefer the works of that scoundrel, that odious, that malignant writer, to the exquisite essays of that angelic creature!' I protested that there was no evidence that angels could write particularly well, but it was in vain, and it was some time before he forgave me. Some of his visitors, who casually encountered peculiarities like these, did not always understand them. But to me he was a man of buoyant sagacity and careless kindness.

There was little to suggest during my MA course that I had any hope, or desire, to become a scholar. I was a dutiful student and respected the niceties in the classical writings; but my own intellect and taste did not lead me in that direction. With a mind apt to wander, I have great difficulty in making a thing complete. My parents gently censured the haste and carelessness in my writing—and my tendency to criticise rather than get to the bottom of a subject. I wrote to my father that I had rather exert my mind very hard for a short time than attend for a long time to a great number of comparatively easy things. This defect of mental constitution made me a suspect observer, for observation implies constant attention to a considerable number of minutiae, which is to me an irksome labour. Many a downtrodden scholar serves up the crumbs of ancient feasts, though well knowing in his heart that they are crumbs. My great concern was to avoid seeming dull, in the manner of the detached historian imprisoned in his tower, insensitive to the immediacy of the encircling world.

Towards the end of my MA, through my university and Unitarian connections, I began writing for the *Prospective Review*, which was then conducted by Martineau and Roscoe. One of my earliest excursions into print was a review of a book on the currency question, which included an article by my future father-in-law Mr James Wilson, proprietor of *The Economist*. The essay satisfied the journal and led to an invitation to review Mill's *Principles of Political Economy*, which I found rather dreary, despite the admirable qualities of mind displayed in it. As I said at the time, Mill belonged to the unspiritual order of great thinkers, who never assumed the teachings of conscience. He never, that is, treated as primordial facts either the existence of a law of duty independent of consequences, nor a moral government of the world. He had a wonderful skill in applying comprehensive principles to complicated phenomena and the power of exhausting a subject like Aristotle or Bentham. But whatever his merits or deficiencies, his great characteristic was that the light of his intellect was exactly what Bacon calls 'dry light'; it was 'unsteeped in the humours of the affections'.

My essay on Mill, which appeared in the year of European tumult, took little exception to his economic theories, but his want of a moral dimension lowered my spirits. The most important matters for the labouring classes, as for all others, are restraining discipline over their passions and an effectual culture of their consciences. As I saw it, the moral and physical condition of the poor was a crucial issue in an emergent democracy:

> Whatever be the evil or the good of democracy, in itself it is evident that the combination of democracy, and low wages will infallibly be bad.... Such is the lesson which the annals of Europe in the year 1848 teach English statesmen. The only effectual security against the rule of an ignorant, miserable, and vicious democracy, is to take care that democracy shall be educated, and comfortable and moral. Now is the time for scheming, deliberating and acting. To tell a mob how their condition may be improved is talking hydrostatics to the ocean. Science is of use now because she may be heard and

understood. If she not be heard before democracy come, when it is come her voice will be drowned in the uproar.

What I innocently anticipated in 1848 was that the spread of education would succeed in a few years in increasing the forethought of the labouring classes, thereby providing an obstacle to their recklessness while improving their physical condition.

⚓︎

After I had taken my MA in 1848, the law beckoned. But while I carried out my duties in the chambers of Sir Charles Hall and Mr Justice Quain, both of whom I admired, I came to abhor the prospect of a legal career. The law course, though complex, was tedious; and I had doubts whether special pleading was morally defensible. The same defects in my character that suppressed my desire to be a scholar suppressed my desire to be a lawyer. My power of accumulating knowledge is limited, and requires such express and repeated exertions to yield any fruit, that a lawyer's life would have required from me a more complete absorption than it does from the ordinary mass of successful practitioners. I saw no adequate object to be gained by so complete a devotion. Moreover, the dreary routine, the hot courts, the heavy wigs, the night work of a thriving barrister, would have put my health at risk, leaving little leisure to pursue my wider interests. The law requires incessant attention yet for me was not sustaining. In those days, my mind was given to truths whose course was shadowy and imprecise. While I pursued a legal training these higher half thoughts—half instincts—were being starved. The law usurped the fabric of my brain without utilizing it.

While economic and political questions increasingly engaged my attention, a closer study of the historical evidences of Christianity was unsettling my religious convictions, which had always been more tentative than conclusive. What can be worse for people than to hear in their youth arguments, alike clamorous and endless, founded on ignorant interpretations of inconclusive words? As I arrived at the years of discretion, I had become lazy in believing. My inner life was too harsh and vacant to give me an abiding hold on parts of religion. Because my parents disagreed on many tenets, I was never taught any scheme of doctrine as absolute certainty. I was withdrawing from the inherited beliefs of my childhood, which my mother found disconcerting, but not lapsing into irreligion. Anyone who can understand Hume will not be in a hurry to believe any *irreligious* philosophy.

In religious matters, it is prudent to venerate what we do not comprehend. My collision with the world had led to doubt, but excessive doubt can lead to paralysis. We cannot prove that God is infinite, omnipotent and good, but we require the assumption that He is so or all is dark. But my own primitive religious instincts were stronger than my affections for this or that church. The simple choice for a man is not which faith, but whether he will have any faith at all in a world coming under the antagonistic influence of science. I believed in a transcendent God, but I was becoming sympathetic to the agnostic view that we are incapable of apprehending His mind or purposes. All is shadow, whatever our fancies dream.

Cease, empty Faith, the Spectrum saith,
   I was, and lo, have been;
I, God, am nought: a shade of thought,
   Which, but by darkness seen,
Upon the unknown yourselves have thrown,
   Placed it and light between.

A reasonable but uncertain faith was the orthodoxy I was coming to entertain.

During my legal training, I visited Oxford from time to time to see my friend Constantine Prichard, the son of Dr Prichard and a fellow of Balliol. It was there that I came into contact with a circle of Newman's followers. Several of my friends thought that under the sway of Newman's creed I was moving towards Rome, a move which they greeted with alarm. When an Englishman sees anything in religion which he does not like, he always, prima facie, imputes it to the Pope. The English have ever believed that the Papist is a kind of *creature*; and every sound mind would prefer a beloved child to produce a tail, a hide of hair, and a taste for nuts, in comparison with transubstantiation, wax-candles, and a belief in the glories of Mary.

The Catholic Church advertises itself by its bold pretension; it has authority to speak; it has a lesson to teach, which eager men learn readily, which imaginative men love to hear. As Newman's life bears witness, Catholicism advertises for men with spiritual ambition, and it bids higher than any other creed. It gets rid of the tameness of life, of the poorness of human duties, of the petty definiteness of ordinary existence. A superhuman morality will always be appealing to aspiring youth; they will run to hear it; they will long to obey and practise it. But although the Catholic Church appealed to my moral and historical sensibilities, I dreaded her tendency to use her power over the multitude for purposes of a low ambition. Dogma is a dry hard husk, and Catholics are too ready to believe at command and force their reasonings into a rigid conformity. And in general, those who preside in the sheepfold partake most eminently of the qualities of the wolf.

As a young man, I admired Newman's writings, especially the Oxford sermons and *Lyra Apostolica*; but though impressed by his literary genius and the subtlety of his intricate logic, I came to distrust his dark introspection and disregard for evidence. For all his psychological insight, I thought his power of analysis limited.

He could conceive finer shades of feeling and motive than his conscience would confidently estimate. Although a master of the difficulties in the creeds of other men, he failed to construct a religious system which could carry along those who had a distinct perception of real truth, so that in the end his disciples were left to look with wonder upon the face of doubt.

It was during my law studies that I came to admire Clough, my breakfast companion at Mr Robinson's lodgings, who had come under Newman's influence at Oxford. He had recently resigned his fellowship at Oriel College, and Roscoe and I had been instrumental in his election as Principal of University Hall, a residence attached to University College. Clough was a man of great honesty and moral courage, with immense feeling and a fastidious taste in all moral and intellectual questions. He had a doubting mind and weighed the pros and cons of every idea. '*ACTION will furnish belief*,' he wrote, '—but will that belief be the true one?' The cast of Clough's thought was a sort of truthful scepticism, which stirred in my own mind a suspicion of action. He could not catch up a creed as other men do, nor dissolve the world into credible ideas and then believe in them. He felt that there was an invisible world but shrank in nervous horror from defining it.

Such thoughts were a fertile ground of speculative interest to me at a time when I was given to bouts of melancholy, perplexed by spiritual and philosophical matters and wearied by an exhausted will. 'Since labours' weary curse began/To dog the steps of anxious man', I wrote despairingly. Despite my doubting temper, I sought a rational, consoling creed. Intense convictions make a memory for themselves, and if they can be kept to the truth of which there is good evidence, they give a readiness of intellect, a confidence in action, a consistency of character, which are not to be had without them. But convictions are a private matter. There is much of mankind that a man can only learn from himself. Behind every man's external life, which he leads in company, there is another which he leads alone, and which he carries with him apart. We see but one aspect of our neighbour, as we see but one side of the moon; in either case there is also a dark half, which is unknown to us. We all come down to dinner, but each has a room to himself.

Nothing is such a bore as looking for your principles. Education, like worldly experience, is disillusioning. People who have thought know that inquiry is suffering,

> Must mourn the deepest o'er the fatal truth,
> The Tree of Knowledge is not that of Life.

As I weighed the cost of certainties lost, I took comfort in the Preface to *Endymion*: 'The imagination of a boy is healthy, and the mature imagination of a man is healthy, but there is a space of life between, in which the soul is in a ferment, the character undecided, the way of life uncertain, the ambition thick sighted.' I was fully alive to my own mawkishness and bitterness, the maze which entangles a mind in search of certainty, sensible to the many-sided aspects truth can take, and sought to escape into the daylight.

In my bewilderment, I wrote a gloomy poem on some remarks of Hutton on 'causeless melancholy', which reflected my state of mind in that 'space of life between', when I was confronted with life's mysteries and troubles at home.

> *No* pain is causeless; o'er God's mightiest sons
> Two angels Grief and Guilt divined their sway;
> He who affliction's icy tempest shuns
> Must tread a path where *fouler* breezes stray.
> The heavy steps of sad repentance lie
> Along the burning sands by passion spread,

But they who shrink not from a wintry sky,
  High o'er the Alps of *sinless* sorrow tread.
The pilgrim bent Messiah's land to gain
Must pass a desert, or a mountain chain.

My melancholy search for truth intensified my growing qualms about human motive and precipitous action, which modern passion promotes. We persuade ourselves that what we wish to believe is true, and the stronger the will, the greater the need to satisfy that desire by action. Illusions please, and the tendency of practical life is to provide beliefs that suit practical life; but this does not make them true. Despite my intellectual restlessness, I was coming to suspect over-haste and over-eagerness in public life, what Clough called 'the ruinous force of the will'. Earlier, simpler and more violent ages propelled a predisposition to action unsuited to our time and dangerous to our future. A settled belief in a falsity is easily generated. Despite all the complexity of modern life, men rarely suspend their beliefs; they court precipitancy when suspension of judgment would better suit society. Pascal said that most of the evils of life arose from 'man's being unable to sit still in a room'. I do not go to that length, but it is certain that we should have been a far wiser race than we are if we had been readier to sit still.

❧❀❧

CHAPTER III

A French Experience

I HAD become rather gloom-ridden in London. Like many a man in his twenties who thinks he knows the world, I was too proud in my eager and shifting thoughts to follow Pascal's counsel to sit still in my room. The commonplaceness of life goaded me; placid society irritated me. Like Shelley, hurrying to and fro in a world of sorrow, I was self-absorbed, in search of fresh experience. Myriad thoughts rattled around my addled brain when I visited Paris in the summer of 1851. It was my first trip to the Continent since the summer of 1844, when my Aunt and Uncle Reynolds had escorted me to Belgium, Germany and the Alps to see the antiquities and broaden my mind. My purpose was to change the mental atmosphere, improve my French, and wait upon events. The moment was propitious.

Nothing is so exhilarating to the mind as its association with great events. In Paris, I had the chance to witness a national crisis at first hand—without becoming one of its victims. A brilliant season was under way when I arrived, while the divisions between Legitimists, Socialists, Republicans and Democrats made the political climate extraordinarily exciting for an Englishman with memories of 1848. My teasing maxim at the time was that 'a man's favourite ideas are always wrong'. But there were moments of truth that I should not have known if I had stayed in England. My principal insight, if so self-evident an idea can be thus described, was that Frenchmen are not Englishmen and should not be judged by English standards. This line of thought led to a vision of affairs that has stayed with me ever since—that national character is a deep thing, which determines a nation's politics.

I had been in Paris for some months when the long-awaited *coup d'état* of Louis Napoleon took place. For several days I roamed the streets, climbing over the railings of the Palais Royal and scrambling over the palings and overturned cabs and omnibuses. I took a walk across the barricades one morning and superintended the construction of three of them with as much keenness as if I had been Clerk of the Works. The silence was curious. On the frontier a raging multitude, within the kingdom no one—a woman hurrying home, an old man shrugging his shoulders—all as quiet as the grave. I feared the troops would turn up and I be shot so that Napoleon might rule, or a sour and ferocious Montagnard—the most horrible being to the eye I ever saw— might dispatch me for target practice. Having failed to hire a window to see the capture of the fortress, I retired, but slowly; it is unwise to run in a revolution, but if you go calmly and look English there is no particular danger. The whole operation reminded me of the description of the Porteous mob in *The Heart of Midlothian*. The same discipline, absence of plunder, and in the leaders the same deep hatred and fanaticism. I am pleased to have seen a revolution, but once is enough, as there is a touch of sameness in this kind of sight.

My notion was that the President would hold his own, and that it was necessary and even desirable that he do so, for the Constitution was unworkable and the economy shattered. Even I could not believe in a government of barristers and newspaper editors. I elaborated these views in a series of letters to the

Inquirer, the polite Unitarian weekly to which many in my circle subscribed. In my survey of the grave scenes in France, I introduced a measure of satiric playfulness, what tender minds might describe as cynicism. My wish was to avoid the sin of lifelessness, not simply to inform but to shock by defending the seemingly indefensible, challenging the cherished views of my gentle compatriots and high-minded readers, who, while I was defending Louis Napoleon's actions, were assailing his perfidy. The letters exasperated my friends, who accused me of recklessness over their cups. Mr Robinson, who had a thorough antipathy to anyone with the name Napoleon, denounced my opinions at one of his breakfasts!

While I would no longer wish to be seen as an apologist for the *coup d'état*, which turned out to be yet another illustration of 'the ruinous force of the will' that collapsed into Caesarism, I felt then, as I do now, that the protection of industry and employment is the first duty of government. Louis Napoleon did not set the standard for ethical scrupulosity or disinterested devotedness; veracity has never been the family failing. But whatever his defects, 'Brummagem Boney', as my Parisian friend Madame Mohl called him, had one excellent advantage over other French statesmen—he had never been a professor, or a journalist, or a barrister, or, by taste, a *littérateur*. He had not confused himself with history and did not think in leading articles or long speeches. He was all the better for having spent his youth on the turf instead of in a library and having thus learned the instinctive habit of applied calculation, which is essential to a merchant and useful to a politician. Leading articles and essay eloquence are very good and useful. Yet they can be done without. Not so with all things. The selling of figs, the cobbling of shoes, the manufacturing of nails—these are the essence of life. And let those who would frame the constitution of a country think on these things.

During my time in Paris, I justified Napoleon's despotism along Benthamite lines and pointed to the need for a strong executive and the imposition of force lest anarchy prevail. The pervasive belief of the French commercial class with whom I came into contact was that the nation's social fabric was under threat. The debasing torture of acute apprehension was eating into the crude pleasure of simple lives. I do not doubt that baubles and bracelets are things normally less important than common law and constitutional action. But fear was paralysing life and labour, a fear so intense, whether reasonable or unreasonable, that it would have, ere long, invincibly justified itself. The demand for manufactures, not least the market for silks and luxuries, bonbons and trinkets, keeps the wheels of industry turning, without which the labouring class would have been turned out of work without warning, with horrid suffering as a consequence. It is the odd peculiarity of commercial civilisation that the life, the welfare and the existence of thousands of workers depend on their being paid for doing what seems nothing when done.

Just as the first duty of government is to protect trade and encourage employment, the first duty of society is the preservation of society. By the sound work of old-fashioned generations—by the singular pains-taking of the slumberers in churchyards—by dull care and stupid industry—a certain social fabric is somehow created. People contrive to go out to their work, and to find work to employ them until the evening; thus body and soul are kept together. This is what mankind has to show for its six thousand years of toil and trouble. To keep up this system, we must make sacrifices. Parliaments and liberty, eloquence and leading articles, all are well and good— but they are secondary; at all hazards, mankind must be kept alive. As time goes on, this fabric becomes a tenderer and tenderer thing. Men buy, and sell, and die. The real case for Napoleon was that within weeks of the *coup d'état*, society was no longer living from hand to mouth but felt sure of her next meal.

There are two ideas which must be abandoned in discussing any constitution. The first is the idea of our barbarous English ancestors—now happily banished from all civilized society, but still prevailing in old manor-houses and other curious repositories of mouldering ignorance—which in such arid solitudes is thus expressed: 'Why can't foreigners have Kings, Lords and Commons, like we have? What fools they are.' The second pernicious mistake is, like the former, seldom now held upon system, but so many hold it in bits and fragments, and without system, that it is still rather formidable. I allude to the old idea, which still creeps out in writing and conversation, that politics are simply a subdivision of immutable ethics; that there are certain inalienable rights of men in all places and all times, which are the sole and sufficient foundation of all government.

Burke first taught the world at large that these notions are misleading. In opposition, he declared politics to be a matter of time and place—that institutions are shifting things, to be tried by and adjusted to the shifting conditions of a mutable world—that, in fact, politics are but a piece of business to be determined in every case by the exact exigencies of that case; in plain English—by sense and circumstances. This was a great step in political philosophy, though it now seems the events of 1848 have taken thinking persons further. In that year, the same experiment, the experiment of Liberal and Constitutional Government, was tried in virtually every nation of Europe—with what varying futures and differing results! The effect has been to teach men to know that no absurdity is so great as to imagine the same species of institutions suitable or possible for Scotchmen and Sicilians, for Germans and Frenchmen, for the English and Neapolitans.

In 1848, Europe was in a ferment with the newest ideas, the best theories, the most elaborate and artistic constitutions. There was the labour, toil and trouble of a million intellects, as good perhaps as the world is likely to see—of old statesmen, literary gentlemen and youthful enthusiasts drawn from all over Europe. Well, what did we gain? A parliament in Sardinia! Surely this is a lesson against proposing politics that won't work, convening assemblies that can't legislate, constructing executives that cannot keep the peace, founding constitutions inaugurated with tears and eloquence, soon abandoned with tears and shame. The year of revolutions began with a course of fair auguries and liberal hopes, propelled by a nonsensical belief in the brotherhood of man; it ended in frightened people taking familiar refuge under dictatorships. The failure of 1848 frustrated the democratic development of Europe but illustrated that ideas could not be realized unless one had the means to achieve them.

The Revolution of 1848 and subsequent affairs in France persuaded me that of all the circumstances affecting political problems, by far the most important is *national character*. The formation of this character is one of the most secret of mysteries. Why nations have the character we see them to have is as little explicable to our shallow perspicacity as why individuals, our friends or our enemies, have the character which they have; why one man is stupid and another clever, another volatile and a fourth consistent. These and other similar problems daily crowd on our observation and only do not puzzle us because we are too familiar with their difficulty to dream of attempting their solution. Only this much is certain: all men and all nations have a character, and that character when once taken is, I do not say unchangeable—religion modifies it, catastrophe annihilates it— the least changeable thing in this ever-changeful world.

'Races and their varieties,' says the historian, 'seem to have been created with an inward *nisus* diminishing with the age of the world.' The people of the South are yet the people of the South, fierce and angry as their summer sun—the people of the North are still cold and stubborn like their own north wind—the people of the East 'mark not, but are still'—the people of the West 'are going through the ends of the earth, and walking up and down in it'. The fact is certain, the cause beyond us. The subtle stream of obscure causes, whereby sons and daughters resemble not only their fathers and mothers but even their great-great-grandfathers and great-great-grandmothers, may very likely be destined to be very inscrutable. In history too, nations have one character, one set of talents, one list of temptations, and one duty. There are breeds in the animal man just as in the animal dog. When you hunt with greyhounds and course with beagles, then, and not till then, may you expect the inbred habits of a thousand years to pass away, that Hindoos can be free, or that Englishmen will be slaves.

The most essential mental quality for a free people, whose liberty is to be progressive, permanent, and on a large scale, is what I provocatively call *stupidity*. This paradoxical idea, which I advanced in my letters to the *Inquirer*, was then something of a novelty and a heresy, but I subscribe to it still. Free institutions are apt to succeed with a dull and stupid people and to fail with a ready-witted and vivacious one. Take the Roman character. Are they not, with one notable exception, the great political people of history? Is not a certain dullness their most visible characteristic? What is the history of their speculative mind?—a blank. What their literature?—a copy. They have left not a single discovery in any abstract science; not a single perfect or well-formed work of high imagination. The Greeks, the perfection of narrow and accomplished genius, bequeathed to mankind the ideal forms of self-idolising art—the Roman imitated and admired; the Greeks explained the laws of nature—the Romans wondered and despised; the Greeks invented a system of numerals second only to that now in use the Romans counted to the end of their days with the clumsy apparatus which we still call by their name. Throughout Latin literature this is the perpetual puzzle—why are we free and they slaves?

As I mischievously pronounced in my letters, the English are unrivalled in stupidity, by which I meant the roundabout common sense and dull custom that steers the opinion of most men. Stupidity is a characteristic suited to our carelessly created Constitution and its institutional freedoms. Steady labour and dreary material—wrinkles on the forehead and figures on the tongue—these are what Englishmen admire. Remote ideas do not seize our imaginations and turn us into fanatics. Nor are our cumbrous intellects given to light artificialities. We are not tempted to levity for we do not see the joke. You will hear more wit in an Irish street-row than would keep Westminster Hall in humour for weeks. We do not excel in punctuated detail or nicely squared elaboration. It puts us out of patience that others should. A respectable Englishman murmured in the Café de Paris, 'I wish I had a hunch of mutton'. He could not bear the secondary niceties with which he was surrounded. Our politics has the same principle. We excel in simple realities, in solid food.

A proper stupidity keeps a man from all the defects of cleverness; it chains the gifted possessor mainly to his old ideas. It takes him weeks to comprehend an atom of a new one; it keeps him from being led away by new theories. He is slow indeed to be excited—his passions, his feelings and his affections are dull and tardy, fixed on a certain known object, acting in a moderate degree and at a sluggish pace. You always know where to find his mind. Sir Robert Peel set the standard—the greatest Member of Parliament that ever lived, an absolutely perfect transactor of public business—the type of the nineteenth-century Englishman, as Sir Robert Walpole was of the eighteenth. Was there ever such a dull man? As Tennyson says of Peel in his inimitable description, the man's talk is of truisms and bullocks; his head is replete with rustic visions of mutton and turnips, guano and grain. Notwithstanding, he is the salt of the earth, the best of the

English breed. Who is like him for sound sense? But I must restrain my enthusiasm.

In the faculty of writing nonsense, stupidity is no match for genius. But what we opprobriously call stupidity, though not an enlivening quality in society, is nature's favourite resource for preserving steadiness of conduct and consistency of opinion. It enforces concentration. People who learn slowly learn only what they must. The best security for people's doing their duty is that they should not know anything else to do; the security for fixedness of opinion is that people should be incapable of comprehending what is to be said on the other side. These valuable truths are no discoveries of mine. They are familiar enough to people whose business it is to know them. Hear what a dense and aged attorney says of your peculiarly promising barrister: 'Sharp! oh yes, yes! he's too sharp by half. He is not safe.' 'What style, sir, is to be preferred in the composition of official dispatches?' asked the youthful aspirant for literary renown to a Director of the East India Company. 'My good fellow,' responded the Ruler of Hindustan, 'the style as we like is the Humdrum.' I extend this and advisedly maintain that nations, just as individuals, may be too clever to be practical, and not dull enough to be free. Dullness is the English line, as cleverness is that of the French.

The French have in some manner or other put their mark on all the externals of European life. The essence of every country remains little affected by their teaching; but in all the superficial embellishments of society the French have enjoined the fashion; and the very language in which those embellishments are spoken of shows at once whence they were derived. Something of this is doubtless due to the accidents of a central position, and an early and prolonged political influence; but more to a certain neatness of nature, a certain finish of the senses, which enables the French more readily than others to touch lightly the light things of society, to see the *comme-il-faut*. 'I like', said a good judge, 'to hear a Frenchman talk; he strikes a light.' On a hundred topics he gives the bright, sharp edge, where others have only a blunt approximation. The language of loquacious Gaul has been sharpened and improved by the constant keenness of attentive minds. And a language long employed by a delicate and critical society is a treasure of dexterous felicities. It is crystallized *esprit*.

There is a characteristic aloofness of the Gothic mind, with its tendency to devote itself to what is not present, which is represented in composition by want of care in the pettiness of style. A certain clumsiness pervades all tongues of German origin. In contrast, a Frenchman can't be clumsy; *esprit* is his essence. Wit is to him as water, *bons-mots* as bonbons. He reads and he learns by reading; levity and literature are his line. The essence of the French character is a certain mobility, and excessive sensibility to present impressions; it issues in a postponement of seemingly fixed principles to a momentary temptation of a transient whim. In England obstinacy is the commonest of the vices, and perseverance the cheapest of the virtues, whereas in France, impatience, inconstancy and excitement lead to the sacrifice of old habits to present emergencies.

The result is that the experiment of establishing political freedom in France is now eighty years old, and while the Third Republic shows the prospect of life and growth, it is an experiment still. There have been perhaps half a dozen new French beginnings—half a dozen complete failures since the Constitution of 1791. There exist various and excellent explanations of these failures, but I can't help feeling a suspicion that some common principle is at work in all of these cases—that over and above all these missed opportunities and bankruptcies there is an unfitness for the trade. There is some lurking quality in the character of the French nation which renders them but poorly adapted for the form and freedom and constitution of the state which they have so often, with such zeal and so vainly, attempted to establish.

France is a nation apt to conceive a great design, but unable to persist in its pursuit because it has a morbid appetite for exhaustive and original theories. You will find nothing there but the most lucid and logical deduction of all things actual and possible from a few principles obtained without evidence and retained in defiance of probability. To Frenchmen, deduction is a game and induction a grievance. Clever, impatient people prefer teaching to learning, and instruction expresses at least the alleged possession of knowledge. The easiest way to shorten the painful, the slow and tedious process of preliminary inquiry is to assume a pretty theory. Life is short—art is long—truth lies deep—learning is low—take some side—found some school. It is as necessary for a public writer to have a theory as to have a pen. His course is obvious; he assumes some grand principle—the principle of Legitimacy, or the principle of Equality, or the principle of Fraternity—and thence he reasons down without fear or favour to the details of everyday politics. Events are judged, not by their relation to simple causes, but by their bearing on a remote axiom.

While I resided in Paris, hundreds of able writers debated with the keenest ability and most ample array of generalities whether the country should be governed by a legitimate monarchy, or an illegitimate; by a social, or an old fashioned republic; by a two-chambered constitution, or a one-chambered constitution, on the claims of Louis Napoleon, or the divine right of the national representation. Can any intellectual food more dangerous or more stimulating for an over-excitable population be conceived? It was the same in Parliament, where each member had his scheme for the regeneration of mankind. In the natural factiousness of the French, Orleanist hated Legitimist; Legitimist Orleanist; Republican detested undiluted Republican. Scheme was set against scheme, and theory against theory. No deliberative assembly can exist with every member wishing to lead, and no one wishing to follow. Such abstract reasoning would not manage a parish vestry, much less a great nation. A successful system of government must fit the hearths and homes of men, not the salons of intellectuals. It is easy to compose politics if you neglect this simple truth.

We are left to deal with the French character pretty much as we find it. We must take the data which we have, and not those which we desire or imagine. In my letters I designed to prove that the French were by character unfit for a solely and predominantly parliamentary government. So many great elements of convulsion existed there that it would be clearly necessary that a strong, vigorous, anti-barricade executive should, at whatever risk and cost, be established and maintained. Such an assembly as the last was irreconcilable with this; in a word, that riots and revolutions must, if possible, come to an end, and only such a degree of liberty and democracy be granted to the French nation as was consistent with the consolidated existence of the order and tranquillity which are equally essential to rational freedom and civilized society.

In order to combine the maintenance of order and tranquillity with the maximum of possible liberty, I hoped that it would in the end be found possible to admit into a political system a representative and sufficiently democratic assembly, without that assembly assuming and arrogating to itself nearly omnipotent powers. I earnestly desired to believe that some such system as this would be workable in France. Otherwise, unless I misread history, the essential deficiencies of debating Girondin statesmen would become manifest, the uncompact, unpractical, over-volatile, over-logical, indecisive, ineffectual rule of Gallican parliaments would be unequivocally manifest, and, no medium being held or conceived to be possible, the nation would sink back under the rule of a military despot.

My musings in France had enlivened my spirits, emboldened my thoughts and animated my writing. The letters in the *Inquirer* persuaded me that I could write with some style and originality and was not the wretched observer of my imaginings. They restored my self-confidence and suppressed my self-doubt. I had been miserable living alone in my London lodgings, but I now saw a way to bridge the distance between Langport and London. At first, I thought I could avoid stagnation by combining a literary life with the Bar, but this idea soon became untenable for reasons both personal and professional. The prospect of becoming a rickety, sodden and dispirited member of Lincoln's Inn filled me with horror. I wrote to my father: 'I have been considering carefully the question which we almost decided upon when I was at home. I mean my abandoning the law at the present crisis—and in accordance with what we very nearly resolved upon when I was with you—I have decided to do so at this juncture—utterly and for ever.' It was a decision I have never regretted, for the thickets of the legal maze would have diverted me from the pleasure of writing without the compensation of contentment.

CHAPTER IV

Banking and Letters

B Y the summer of 1852, I was content to return to Somerset and the beauties of Herd's Hill and its lovely garden, which my father had laid out with the eye of an artist. A principal cause of my homecoming was a sense of filial duty, to relieve my father of some of the burden of caring for my mother, who had come to depend on me for support. Contact with insanity had a depressing effect on my nervous system, and my mother's illness had caused me to lead something of a secretive life in London. I had got into the habit of exercising discretion and watching for danger signals. My father's reports of my mother's erratic behaviour were among the alarming realities which haunted the family like a death's head.

A dreamy mind—a mind occupied intensely with its own thoughts—will often have a peculiarly intense apprehension of anything which by hard collision with the world it has been forced to observe. If I had learned anything from Clough, whose critical mind had led him to a morbid sensibility, it was to take this world lightly, to try to live quietly, but openly, and see what truth would come. My dreaminess and high spirits provided something of a defence against spectral scares and depression. But thinking back on that painful time with my mother, whose future seemed destined to be spent outside society, I struggled to avoid becoming a victim of despair. The torments of youth are rarely dignified and a lingering melancholy and reserve resulted from my distress over my mother's condition. Every trouble in life is a joke compared to madness.

***

In England a position in the world is necessary for comfort. As the son of a prosperous family, I had the material expectations of such an upbringing. The life of an idle provincial gentleman held out little charm for someone of my temper; there is a sickly incompleteness about people too fine for the world, and too nice to work their way in it. But having abandoned a legal career and without a military or clerical background, I had few professional prospects. The life of a writer appealed, but the quiet of the study lacks the excitement of the street, the sense of coping with the immediacy of tangible reality. Moreover, a passive and leisurely life at home would have left me brooding all the more over my mother. Unlike the dryness of the law, I thought, the world of business offered a better balance to the subjects that I had come to enjoy and wished to pursue. The daily routine offered an escape from domestic cares, while offering a breadth of experience which I felt was lacking in so much literary production.

So many poor books are written because writers have so little knowledge of the world outside their studies. With the exception of poetry, secluded habits do not tend to eloquence; and the apathy so common in studious persons is exceedingly unfavourable to the liveliness of narration and illustration which is needed for excellence in even the simpler forms of writing. Moreover, it will perhaps be found that persons devoted to mere literature commonly become devoted to mere idleness. They wish to produce a great work, but they find they cannot; they wish to write, but nothing occurs to them. Unless they are very poor, their lives have no events. With any decent means of subsistence, they have nothing to rouse them from an indolent and musing dream. A merchant must meet his bills, or is civilly dead and uncivilly remembered. But a student may know nothing of time and be too lazy to wind up his watch. 'Went into the parlour and tied on my shoe-buckles,' said the retired citizen in Addison's *Spectator*. This is the sort of life for which studious men commonly relinquish the pursuits of business and the society of their fellows.

Every parent believes in the hereditary principle, and the principle has paid regular dividends to me over the years. Just as the miner's son is destined for the pit and the butcher's boy for the shop, I was destined for the Stuckey Bank, which had expanded over the years under my uncle's direction and boasted various branches in Somerset and an office in London. A position was on offer, which resolved the issue of employment. Work at the Bank was agreeable in theory but irksome in practice. I approve of the mercantile life, but a love of poetry is poor preparation for double entry book-keeping. My habitual difficulty in attending to detail and my inability to 'add up', despite being the 'family wrangler', initially alarmed my punctilious father, who in the business of banking maintained a scrupulous solemnity.

I sinned against the conventions of mercantile existence by treating them in a light and flippant manner, preferring short cuts to the customary modes of conduct. I felt no pleasure in making money, and the processes of the business mind bored me. I maintained in vain that sums are matters of opinion, but the people in command at the Bank did not comprehend the nature of contingent matter and insisted that figures tend to one result more than another. Still, any careful person who is experienced in figures, and has real sound sense, may easily make himself a good banker. The modes in which money can be safely lent are not many, and a clear-headed, quiet, industrious person may soon learn all that is necessary about them. Having passed some time in an attorney's office, I was well acquainted with all the petty technicalities which intellectual men in middle life in general cannot learn. There is an inscrutable something which at once and altogether distinguishes the man who is safe in the affairs of life from those who are unsafe. If I have been successful in banking it has been more through intuition than application, in seizing the main issues of a question with assurance.

The bustling world of banking is an unlikely backdrop to the writing of metaphysics. Happily, it is a watchful, not an arduous, trade, which gave scope for real intimacy with the things that exercised my mind in those days. A banker, even in a large business, can feel pretty sure that all his transactions are sound, and yet have much spare mind. My spare mind, divided since childhood between the competing worlds of commerce and literature, sought to reconcile the busy life of men of affairs and the lonely rapture of Attic sages. If you would vanquish earth, you must invent heaven. I found it in conversation—the genial exchange of prejudice among friends—and in writing. I never tire of repeating that you can't write without having something to say, and you can't have anything worth saying without catching ideas from contact with your fellow-creatures on lines which have a stirring interest to you and to them. I not only enjoyed the intellectual companionship of my friends, but also mingled with the rural folk of Somerset for a ready source of supine sagacity. No educated mind can, without experience, divine the ideas of the uneducated.

Composition is pleasant work for men of ready words, fine ears and thick-coming illustrations which run out from the riches of their literary memory. Like other voracious readers, I found compensation in the excitement of writing. But while I sought new prospects in literature, my own slight vein of poetry was exhausted. It seems to be a law of the imagination that poetry only works in a mind of stillness. The noise and crush of life jar it. 'No man', it has been said, 'can say, I *will* compose poetry.' He must wait until—from a brooding half-desultory inaction—poetry may arise, like a gentle mist, delicately and of itself. Like the French whom I mocked, I had my own tendency to 'cleverness', which is better suited to prose than to verse. Variety is my taste and versatility my weakness. My wandering mind found a vehicle in writing articles and reviews for the quarterlies, where I could express my opinions on literature, history and politics with the noise and crush of life on my doorstep. In keeping with my view that national character determines the political life of a nation, I assumed in my literary and biographical essays that character determines the life of an individual, that temperament is fate.

My own imagination acts like a seizure, and on the train journeys between Taunton, Bristol and London and the long evenings at Herd's Hill, ideas whirled around my restive brain. In my literary guise, my ambition was to avoid the tyranny of the commonplace that seems to accompany civilization, to recapture the bold humour and the explicit statement of former days. People dread to be thought unsafe in proportion as they get their living by being thought to be safe. The secret of prosperity in common life is to be commonplace in principle, but the commonplace is death to literature and the *art* of conversation. 'Literary men', it is said, 'are outcasts; they can say strong things of their age; for no one expects they will go out and act on them.' They are a kind of ticket-of-leave lunatics, from whom no harm is for the moment expected; who *seem* quiet, but on whose vagaries a practical public must have its eye. To expect them to *be* quiet would be as reasonable as to expect the art of walking to disappear.

I began a series of articles on the English classics, which did not require arduous research and could be accomplished with a certain *je ne sais quoi*. I was persuaded that the most perfect books have been written not by those who thought much of books, but by those who thought little, by those who were under the restraint of a sensitive talking world, to which books had contributed something, and a varied, eager life the rest. Literature is my pastime and pleasure, and my essays on Béranger and Bishop Butler, Shakespeare and Milton, Shelley and Hartley Coleridge, Cowper and Scott, fulfilled a desire without requiring scientific rigour. I had hunting, banking, publishers, Christmas and an article to do all at once, and it was my opinion they would all get muddled. But a muddle will print, though it won't add up—*which is the real advantage of literature.*

My earliest literary essays appeared in the *Prospective Review*, which suffered from a somewhat narrow and sectarian tendency of advanced Socinianism. It did not prosper, and in 1855 Hutton and I founded the *National Review*, which Hutton edited with my occasional interventions. Its purpose was to cover an 'open field', as Martineau put it, of unrepresented opinion between the heavy Whiggism and decorous latitudinarianism of the *Edinburgh* and the arid radicalism of the *Westminster*. Its circulation, much of it in the United States, was modest, but it provided a diversion from the routine at the Bank, introduced me to the world of letters, and gave me ample space to exercise my literary judgment. My mind is inaccessible to the contagion of blind sympathy, and in my reviews I took the view that the business of the critic is criticism; it is *not* his business to be thankful; he must attempt an estimate rather than a eulogy.

I am ever mindful of the charge that reviewing is for the lazy and superficial, which so often subjects readers, as Hazlitt said, to the slow torture of tedious extracts. Reviewing appears a tiresome mode of stating opinions, and a needless confusion of personal facts with abstract arguments. Some, especially authors who have been censured, say that it is easier to write a review than a book and that reviewers are, as Coleridge declared, a species of maggots, inferior to bookworms, living on the delicious brains of real genius. Doubtless it is easier to write one review than one book, but not many reviews than one book. In my own defence, I republished some of my studies in 1858, under the title *Estimates of Some Englishmen and Scotchmen*, a volume which received mixed notices—praise from Matthew Arnold and ridicule elsewhere—but which gave me the vain but harmless pleasure of seeing my name on a book. It acquitted me of the charge of laziness, though it failed to elevate me to the rank of genius.

For me, as an Englishman, the best literature is the English, and thus my subjects came mostly from home. We understand the language; the manners are familiar, the associations our own. Of course, a man who has not read Homer is like a man who has not seen the ocean. But we cannot be always looking out to sea. We stop and gaze; we look and wonder at the other world, but we live onshore. The use of foreign literature is like the use of foreign travel. It imprints on us in early and susceptible years a deep sense of strange and noble objects. But they do not resemble our familiar life; they do not bind themselves to our intimate affection; they are picturesque and striking, like strangers and wayfarers, but they are not of our home and cannot touch the hearth of the soul. It would be better to have no outlandish literature in the mind than to have it the principal thing. We should be like accomplished vagabonds without a country, like men with a hundred acquaintances and no friends. We need an intellectual possession analogous to our own life, on which we can repose. Let us be thankful if our researches in foreign literature enable us better to comprehend our own.

In my literary essays style was a preoccupation, my own as well as that of the writers under review. Hazlitt—that fertile and furious critic—said that to write in a genuine, familiar English style was to write as one would speak in common conversation but with a thorough command and choice of words, setting aside all pedantic and oratorical flashes. Many people have offered theories of literary composition, but I believe that the knack in style is to write like a human being, to be oneself. Some think they must be wise, some elaborate, some concise. Plato wrote like a seer; Tacitus like a pair of stays; Carlyle like a comet, inscribing with his tail. But legibility is given to those who neglect these notions and are willing to be themselves, who express their thoughts in the simplest words, in the words wherein they were thought. Rhythm should animate literary composition but should not protrude upon the surface, nor intrude upon the attention. It should be a latent charm, though a real one.

A writer of genius, like a great man of the world, is distinguished by what I call 'animated moderation'. His writings are never slow or exaggerated; they combine instinct with judgment, and yet that judgment is never dull; they have as much spirit in them as would go to make a wild writer, and yet every line of them is the product of a sane and sound writer. The best and almost perfect instance of this in English is Scott. Homer was perfect in it, as far as we can judge; Shakespeare is often perfect in it for long together, though then, from the defects of a bad education and a vicious age, all at once he loses himself in excesses. Still, Homer, and Shakespeare at his best, and Scott, though in other respects so unequal to them, have this remarkable quality in common—this union of life with measure, of spirit with reasonableness.

English literature undoubtedly contains much impurity of style, if not meaning; but it also contains one nearly perfect model of the pure style in the literary expression of typical *sentiment*. Wordsworth comes as near to purity of style in sentiment as is possible. He was vouchsafed the last grace of the self-denying artist; you think neither of him nor his style, but you cannot help thinking of—you *must* recall—the exact phrase, the *very* sentiment he wished, as in 'The Trossachs' or 'Upon Westminster Bridge'. The great subjects of the two sonnets—the religious aspect of beautiful but grave nature—the religious aspect of a city about to awaken and be alive—are the only ideas left in our mind. Instances of a barer style may be found, but few of a purer one. If we take out the description of the brilliant yellow of autumn— 'October's workmanship to rival May'—or the phrase 'This city now doth, like a garment, wear/The beauty of the morning', they have independent value, but they are not noticed in the sonnet when we read it through; they fall into place there, and being in their place, are not seen.

Writing naturally and imaginatively—with spirit and measure—were my aims in my literary essays, concentrating on the lives of the writers as much as the character of the writings. Some sceptics doubt whether it is possible to deduce anything about an author from his works. Yet surely people do not keep a tame steam engine to write their books; and if those books were really written by a man he must have been a man who could write them. The difficulty is the defect of the critics. It is absurd to say, as the experts aver, that we know nothing about Shakespeare, for we have the sure testimony of his writings, which could only be produced by a first-rate imagination working on a first-rate experience. One can deduce from his imagery something of what he has seen. The passage in *Venus and Adonis* which describes a hare running through a flock of sheep to put the hounds off the scent could only have been written by a man who had been hunting. What truly indicates excellent knowledge is the habit of constant, sudden and almost unconscious allusion, which implies familiarity, for it can arise from that alone—and this species of incidental, casual and perpetual reference to 'the mighty world of eye and ear', is the particular characteristic of Shakespeare.

What I sought to illuminate in my literary essays was the art of self-delineation, by which writers leave their readers with an image of themselves. Thus I gave emphasis to Shakespeare's experiencing nature and glancing genius. His imagination always seems to be floating between the contrast of things; and if his mind had a resting place that it liked, it was the ordinary view of extraordinary events. Elsewhere in my literary essays I empha-sized Milton's austere goodness and moral tenacity but want of common sympathy and humour; Sterne's descriptive powers and pagan indecency; Thackeray's irritable sensibility and ever-painful sense of self. There is hardly a work of Hartley Coleridge—the perennial child who 'lost the race he never ran'—or Cowper—whose poetry is autobiography in disguise—which does not contain a finished picture of the writer. All writing, it may be said—even that of the lowly critic—is a form of memoir.

Few poets have left a clearer image of themselves in their writings than Shelley—whose fine fragments, casual expressions of single inspirations, have found a place in a corner of my mind to be served up as garnish to writing and conversation. Few poets have been so artful in getting outside themselves, to contemplate their own character as a fact and to describe it and the movement of their own actions as external forms and images. Every line of his has a personal impress, an unconscious inimitable manner. The peculiarity of his opinions grew out of his temperament. In every delineation we see the same simple intense being, a beau-tiful mind deficient in a sense of duty, without a haunting idea of right or wrong, and an easy abandon in place of a severe self-scrutiny. In Shelley we have a most remarkable instance of the pure impulsive character.

Shelley's predominant impulse was 'a passion for reforming mankind'. He would have been ready to preach that mankind should be 'free, equal, pure, and wise' in the Ottoman Empire, or to the Czar, or to George III. Such truths were independent of time and place and circumstance. It was this undoubting confi-dence which irritated the sceptical Hazlitt, who saw him as a shrill-voiced philosophic fanatic, undisturbed by realities and earthbound feelings. There is no difficulty in imagining Shelley cast by the accident of fortune into the Paris of the Revolution; hurried on by its ideas, not doubting its hopes, wild with its excitement, going forth in the name of freedom, conquering and to conquer. And who can think that he would have been scrupulous in how he attained such an end? It was in him to have walked towards it over seas of blood. One could almost identify him with Saint-Just, the 'fair-haired republican'.

The evidence of Shelley's poems confirms this impression of him. The characters which he delineates have all this same kind of pure impulse. The reforming impulse is especially felt. In almost every one of his works there is some character of whom all we know is that he or she has this passionate disposition to reform mankind. We know nothing else about them, and they are all the same. Laon, in *The Revolt of Islam*, does not differ at all from Lionel, in *Rosalind and Helen*. Laon differs from Cythna, in the former poem, only as male from female. In his more didactic poems it is the same. All the world is evil, and will be evil, until some unknown conqueror shall appear—a teacher by rhapsody and a conqueror by words—who shall at once reform all evil. Such impersonations are, of course, not real men; they are mere incarnations of a desire.

It is most dangerous to be possessed with an idea, and no personal purity is a protection against insatiable zeal. The less a man is conscious of inferior motives, the more likely is he to fancy that he is doing God's service. With Shelley, there is no *caput mortuum* of worn-out threadbare experience to serve as ballast to his mind; it is all volatile, intellectual salt-of-tartar, that refuses to combine its evanescent, inflammable essence with anything solid or anything lasting. Bubbles are to him the only realities—touch them and they vanish. Curiosity is the only proper category of his mind; and though a man of knowledge, he is a child in feeling. The high intellectual impulses which animated him are too incorporeal for human nature; they begin in buoyant joy, they end in eager suffering. The nightshade is more common in his poems than the daisy.

Nothing to Shelley was inevitable or fixed; he fancied he could alter it all. His sphere is the 'unconditional'; he floats away into an imaginary Elysium or an expected Utopia; beautiful and excellent, but having nothing in common with the absolute laws of the present world. Wordsworth describes the world as we know it: where there are moors and hills, where the lichen grows and the slate juts out. Shelley describes the universe. He rushes among the stars; this earth is an assortment of imagery, he uses it to deck some unknown planet. He scorns 'the smallest light that twinkles in the heavens'. His theme is the vast, the infinite, the immeasurable. He is not of our home, nor homely; he describes not our world, but that which is common to all worlds—the Platonic idea of a world. Where it can, his genius soars from the concrete and real into the unknown, the indefinite and the void.

Wordsworth said that in workmanship Shelley was one of the best of us. Macaulay remarked that he had many of the qualities of the ancient masters. The peculiarity of his style is its intellectuality, and this strikes us the more from its contrast with his impulsiveness. He has something of this in life. He was hurried away by sudden desires, as he was in his choice of ends; we are struck with a certain comparative measure and adjustment in his choice of means. So too in his writings. Over the most intense excitement, the grandest objects, the keenest agony, the most buoyant joy, he throws an air of subtle mind. His language is minutely and acutely searching; at the dizziest height of meaning the keenness of the words is greatest. It was from Plato and Sophocles that he gained the last perfection in preserving the accuracy of the intellect when treating of the objects of the imagination; but in its essence it was a peculiarity of his own nature. As it was the instinct of Byron to give in glaring words the gross phenomena of evident objects, so it was that of Shelley to refine the most inscrutable with the curious nicety of an attenuating metaphysician. In the wildest of ecstasies his self-anatomising intellect is equal to itself.

⁂

My excursions into literature brought home to me that we now live in an age of prose, for English poetry has never fully recovered from the eruption which it made at the beginning of this century into the fashionable world. The poems of Lord Byron and Thomas Moore were received with an avidity that resembles our present avidity for sensation novels, and were read by a class which at present reads little but such novels. Old men who remember may be heard to say, 'we hear nothing of poetry now-a-days; it seems quite down'. And 'down' it certainly is. A stray schoolboy may still be detected in a wild admiration for the *Giaour* or the *Corsair*, but the real posterity—the quiet students of a past literature—never read them or think of them. If today a dismal poet were, like Byron, to lament the fact of his birth, and to hint that he was too good for the world, the reviewers would say that a sulky poet was a questionable addition to a tolerable world; that he need not have been born, as far as they were concerned. Doubtless there is much in Byron besides his dismal exaggeration, but it was that exaggeration which made 'the sensation' which gave him a wild moment of dangerous fame. As so often happens, the cause of momentary fashion is the cause of lasting oblivion.

The era of Byron and Moore is forgotten and almost the sole result of the poetry of their day is the harm it has done. It degraded for a time the whole character of the art. It is said that in practice the aim and duty of poetry is to catch the attention of the passing and fashionable world. It fixes upon the minds of a generation that poetry is but one of the many amusements for the enjoying classes, a light literature for the lighter hours, a metrical species of the sensational novel. The mere notion, the bare idea, that poetry is a deep thing, a teaching thing, the most surely and wisely elevating of human things, is even now to the coarse public mind nearly unknown. As is the fate of poetry, so inevitably is that of criticism. When poetry was noisy, criticism was loud; now poetry is a still small voice, and criticism must be smaller and stiller. Years ago when criticism only tried to show how poetry could be made a good amusement, it was not impossible that criticism itself should be amusing. But now it must at least be serious, for poetry is a profound and serious thing.

It is singularly characteristic of this age that the illustrious poems which rise to the surface—those by Tennyson and Browning are conspicuous—should be examples of ornate and grotesque art, which distracts the senses with gay confusion while abstracting the mind from reality. We live in the realm of the half-educated. The number of readers grows daily, but the quality of readers, who consume modern literature like sandwiches on a railway journey, does not improve. The middle class is scattered, headless; it is well meaning, but aimless, wishing to be wise, but ignorant how to be so. The aristocracy in England never was a literary aristocracy; never in the days of its full power—of its unquestioned predominance—did it even seriously try to guide the taste of England.

Without guidance the young are thrown amongst a mass of books; many of them would like to improve their culture, to chasten their taste, if only they knew how. But left to themselves they take, not pure art, but showy art; not that which permanently relieves the eye but glaring art which catches and arrests the eye for a moment. The tired and hasty reader soon moves on to some new excitement, which in its turn stimulates for an instant, and then is passed by for ever. These conditions are not favourable to the due appreciation of pure art—of that art which must be known before it is admired—which must have fastened

on the brain before you appreciate it—which you must love ere it
will seem worthy of your love.

A flashy and grotesque literature seems to be fated to us in
our levelling and restless culture, growing incoherent in the
cacophony of discordant voices. It is our curse, as other times had
theirs.

Come Poet, come!
In vain I seem to call. And yet
Think not the living times forget,
Ages of heroes fought and fell
That Homer in the end might tell;
O'er grovelling generations past
Upstood the Doric fane at last;
And countless hearts on countless years
Had wasted thoughts, and hopes, and fears,
Rude laughter and unmeaning tears;
Ere England Shakespeare saw, or Rome
The pure perfection of her dome.
Others, I doubt not, if not we,
The issue of our toils shall see;
Young children gather as their own
The harvest that the dead had sown,
The dead forgotten and unknown.

The shifting, varied scene of men—their hopes, fears, anxieties, maxims, actions—presents a sight more interesting to man
than any other which has ever existed, and it may be viewed in all
moods of mind, and with the change of inward emotion as the
external object seems to change. Among the most remarkable of
these varied views is the world's view of itself. The world, such as
it is, has made up its mind what it is. Childishly deceivable by
charlatans on every other subject—imposed on by pedantry, by

new and unfound science, by ancient and unfounded reputation, a prey to pomposity, overrun with recondite fools, ignorant of all else—society knows itself. A certain tradition pervades the world, a discipline of the market-place teaches what the collective society of men has ever been, and what, so long as the nature of man is the same, it cannot and will not cease to be.

Literature, the written expression of human nature in every variety, takes up this variety likewise. Ancient literature exhibits it from obvious causes in a more simple manner than modern literature can. Those who are brought up in times like the present necessarily hear a different set of opinions, fall in with other words, and under the shadow of a higher creed. In consequence they cannot have the simple innocence of the old world, that classical blend of intellectual adventure with moral conservatism; they cannot speak with easy equanimity of the fugitiveness of life, the necessity of death, of good as a mean, of sin as an extreme. Still, the spirit of Horace is alive, and as potent as that of any man. In every age there are writers who give expression to what may be called the poetry of equanimity, that is the world's view of itself; its self-satisfaction, its conviction that you must bear what comes, not hope for much, never be excited, admire little and then you will be at peace. This creed does not sound attractive in description. The mind of man, when its daily maxims are put before it, revolts from anything so stupid, so mean, so poor.

It requires a consummate art to reconcile men in print to that moderate philosophy which creeps into all hearts, colours all speech, influences all action. We may not stiffen common sense into a creed; our very ambition forbids:

> *Calm's not life's crown, though calm is well.*
> 'Tis all perhaps which man acquires,
> But 'tis not what our youth desires.

Still, an artist like Arnold may succeed in making 'calm' interesting. Equanimity has its place in literature. Gray's *Elegy*—so
grave and so wise a meditation on death and life—perhaps
remains our most popular English poem. The poetry of equipoise
is possible, though no modern nation can produce art embodying
this kind of cool reflection and delineation as it was once
produced. It has become the victim of our desires and agitations
in a culture given to the transient and glaring, when the theory of
the universe has ceased to be an open question.

CHAPTER V

History

I HAD settled back into a familiar pattern of life at Herd's Hill, which I was content to see continue until something more enticing turned up. My mother desired a daughter-in-law to turn up, but Langport was not richly endowed with young ladies worthy of her expectations. Nor, it might be said, was a lettered banker of whimsical temper considered a great catch by other expectant mothers and their little blue and pink daughters, so like each other. As Hutton said drily, I would have found them more attractive had I not been so short-sighted! With few distractions, I took comfort by the evening fire, mending my pens and turning over my thoughts. In 1856, in addition to the essay on Shelley and another on the character of Sir Robert Peel, I published a series of playful commentaries in the *Saturday Review*. One celebrated the dull and torpid character of English government; another teased the Tories, whose plain creed in those days was the status quo, but who lacked the mastery of principles necessary for their exposition of doing nothing.

As an historian by inclination, if not by trade, I took the opportunity to probe into the character and writings of Gibbon and Macaulay in extended essays in the *National Review*. History, it has been said, is just a succession of calamities without pattern or meaning. Voltaire observed that 'L'histoire n'est que le tableau des crimes et des malheurs', which Gibbon rephrased in his depiction of the past as 'a register of the crimes, follies, and misfortunes of mankind'. A great critic not long ago alleged that historical writings did not establish a theory of the universe, and were therefore of no avail. Yet, as Tocqueville observed, 'history is a gallery of pictures in which there are few originals and many copies'. Even when mankind does not wish to replicate the past, which is rare in human history, the past is not readily left behind.

Whatever may be the use of history in itself, it is certainly of great use to literary men. Consider a man of that species. He sits beside a library fire, with nice white paper, a good pen, a capital style, and nothing to describe. Of course he is an able man, and of course has an active intellect and a wonderful culture; but still one cannot always have original ideas. Every day cannot be an era; a train of new speculation very often will not be found; and how dull it is to make it our business to write, to stay by ourselves in a room to write, and then have nothing to say! It is dreary work mending pens and waiting for a theory to 'turn up'. What a gain if something should happen! Then one could describe it. Something, of course, *has* happened, and that something is history. Since a remarkably grave Greek discovered this plan for a serious immortality, a series of accomplished men have seldom been found wanting to derive literary capital from their active and barbarous kindred. When a Visigoth broke a head, he thought that that was the end of it. Not so: he was making history, and historians write it down.

The manner of writing history is as characteristic of the narrator as the actions are of the persons who have performed them. It may be generally defined as a view of one age taken by another; a picture of a series of men and women painted by one of another series. Of course, this definition seems to exclude contemporary history; but if we look into the matter carefully, is there such a thing? What are all the best and most noted works that claim the title—memoirs, scraps, materials—composed by men of like passions with the people they speak of, involved it may be in the events they speak of, and therefore describing them with the partiality and narrowness of an eager actor; or even worse, by men far apart from them in a monkish solitude, familiar with the lettuces of the convent-garden, but hearing only faint dim murmurs of the great transactions which they slowly jot down in the barren chronicle? These are not to be named in the same short breath with the equable, poised, philosophic narrative of the retrospective historian. In the great histories there are two topics of interest—man as a type of the age in which he lives, and the events and manners of the age he is describing; very often almost all the interest is the contrast of the two.

You should do everything, said Lord Chesterfield, in minuet time. It was in that time that Gibbon wrote his history, and such was the manner of the age. You fancy him in a suit of flowered velvet, with a bag and sword, wisely smiling, composedly rounding his periods. You seem to see the grave bows, the formal politeness, the finished deference. You perceive the minuetic action accompanying the words: 'Give', it would say, 'Augustus a chair: Zenobia, the humblest of our slaves: Odoacer, permit me to correct the defect in your attire.' As the slap-dash sentences of a rushing critic express the hasty impatience of modern manners, so the deliberate emphasis, the slow acumen, the steady argument, the impressive narration bring before us what is now a tradition, the picture of the correct eighteenth-century gentleman, who never failed in a measured politeness, partly because it was due in propriety towards others, and partly because from his own dignity it was due most obviously to himself.

There is not one of the many literary works produced in the eighteenth century more thoroughly characteristic of it than

Gibbon's history. The special characteristic of that age is a clinging to the definite and palpable; it had a taste beyond everything for what it called solid information. In literature, the period may be defined as that in which men ceased to write for students, and had not begun to write for women. In the present day no one can take up any book intended for general circulation without clearly seeing that the writer supposes most of his readers will be ladies or young men; and, in proportion to his judgment, he attends to their taste accordingly. Two or three hundred years ago books were written for professed and systematic students—chief among them college fellows—who used to go on studying them all their lives.

Between these two eras, there was a time in which literary consumers were strong-headed practical men. Education had not become so general, or so feminine, as to make the present style— what is called the 'brilliant style'—at all necessary. But there was enough culture to make the demand of common diffused persons more effectual than that of special and secluded scholars. A book-buying public had arisen of sensible men, who would not endure the awful folio style in which the schoolmen wrote. The business of that age was perhaps more free from the hurry and distraction which disable so many of our practical men at the present time from reading. You accordingly see in the books of the last century what is called a masculine tone; a firm, strong, perspicuous narration of matter of fact, a plain argument, a contempt for everything which distinct definite people cannot entirely and thoroughly comprehend.

There is no more solid book in the world than Gibbon's history. Only consider the chronology. It begins with the year ONE, and goes down to the year 1453, and is a schedule of important events during that time. Scarcely any fact deeply affecting European civilisation is wholly passed over. Laws, dynasties, churches, barbarians, appear and disappear. Everything changes; the old world—the classical civilisation of form and definition—passes away, a new world of free spirit and inward growth emerges; between the two lies a mixed weltering interval of trouble and confusion, when everybody hates everybody, and the historical student leads a life of skirmishes, is oppressed with broils and feuds. All through this long period Gibbon's history goes with steady consistent pace; like a Roman legion through a troubled country—*haeret pede pes*; up and down hill, through marsh and thicket, through Goth or Parthian—the firm defined array passes forward—a type of order and an emblem of civilisation. Whatever may be the defects of Gibbon's history, none can deny him a proud precision and a style in marching order.

Grave, tranquil, decorous pageantry is a part of the essence of the last age. There is nothing more characteristic of Gibbon. A kind of pomp pervades him. He is never out of livery. He selects for narration those themes which look most like a levée: grave chamberlains seem to stand throughout; life is a vast ceremony, the historian at once the dignitary and the scribe. The very language of Gibbon shows these qualities. His majestic march through history has been the admiration of all perusers. It has the greatest merit of an historical style: it is always going on; you feel no doubt of its continuing in motion. But at the same time, the manner of the *Decline and Fall* is about the last which should be recommended for strict imitation. It is not a style in which you can tell the truth. A monotonous writer is suited only to monotonous matter. Truth is of various kinds—grave, solemn, dignified, petty, low, ordinary; and a historian who has to tell the truth must be able to tell what is vulgar as well as what is great, what is little as well as what is amazing.

Gibbon is at fault here. He *cannot* mention Asia Minor. The petty order of sublunary matters; the common gross existence of ordinary people; the necessary littlenesses of necessary life, are little suited to his sublime narrative. Gibbon omits what does not suit him; and the consequence is, that though he has selected the most various of historical topics, he scarcely gives you an idea of variety. The ages change, but the varnish of the narration is the same. It is not unconnected with this fault that he gives us but an indifferent description of individual character. People seem a good deal alike—every man a statue. The cautious scepticism of his cold intellect, which disinclined him to every extreme, depreciates great virtues and extenuates great vices. He cannot be numbered among the great painters of human nature, for he has no sympathy with the heart and passions of our race. He has no place among the felicitous describers of detailed life, for his subject is too vast for minute painting, and his style too uniform for a shifting scene. But he is entitled to a high—perhaps to a first—place among the orderly narrators of great events; the composed expositors of universal history; the tranquil artists who have endeavoured to diffuse a cold polish over the warm passions and desultory fortunes of mankind.

Practical people have little idea of the practical ability required to write a history, especially a large history like Gibbon's. Long before you get to the pen, there is an immensity of pure business; heaps of material are strewn everywhere; but they lie in disorder, unread, uncatalogued, unknown. It seems a dreary waste of life to be analysing, indexing, extracting works and passages, in which one per cent of the contents are interesting, and not half of that percentage will ultimately appear in the flowing narrative. As an accountant takes up a bankrupt's books filled with confused statements of ephemeral events, charges this to that head, and that to this; so the great narrator, going over the scattered annalists of extinct ages, groups and divides, notes and combines, until from a crude mass of darkened fragments there emerges a clear narrative, a concise account of the result and upshot of the whole.

In this art Gibbon was a master. The laborious research of German scholarship, the keen eye of theological zeal, a century of steady criticism has found few faults of detail. The account has been worked right, the proper authorities consulted, an accurate judgment formed, the most telling incidents selected. Such effort of composition is easier with respect to ancient than with respect to modern times. The barbarians burned the books. Although all historians abuse them for it, in their hearts they are greatly rejoiced. If the books had existed, they would have had to read them. Macaulay has to peruse every book printed with long f's; and it is no use after all; somebody will find some stupid MS, an old account-book of an 'ingenious gentleman', and with five entries therein destroy a whole hypothesis. But Gibbon was exempt from this; he could count the books the splendid Goths bequeathed; and when he had mastered them he might pause. Still it is no light matter, as anyone who looks at the books— awful folios in the grave Bodleian—will most certainly credit and believe.

The nature of his authorities clearly shows the nature of Gibbon's work. History may be roughly divided into universal and particular; the first being the narrative of events affecting the whole human race, at least the main historical nations, the narrative of whose fortunes is the story of civilisation; and the latter being the narrative of events in one or two nations only. Universal history comprises great areas of space and long periods of time. There is no instantaneous transmission in historical causation; a long interval is required for universal effects. Universal necessarily partakes of the character of a summary. You cannot recount the cumbrous annals of long epochs without condensation, selection and omission. What this gains in time, it loses in power. The particular history, confined within narrow limits, can show us the whole contents of these limits, explain features of human interest, recount in graphic detail all interesting transactions, touch the human heart with the power of passions, instruct the mind by citing patient instances of accurate wisdom. The universal is confined to a dry enumeration of superficial transactions; no action can have all its details; the canvas is so crowded that no figure has room to display itself effectively.

From the nature of the subject, Gibbon's history is of the latter class. The sweep of the narrative is so wide, the decline and fall of the Roman Empire being in some sense the most universal event which has ever happened—being, that is, the historical incident which has most affected all civilised men, and the very existence and form of civilisation itself—that it is evident that we must look rather for a comprehensive generality than a telling minuteness of delineation. The history of a thousand years does not admit the pictorial detail which a Scott or a Macaulay can accumulate on the history of a hundred. Gibbon has done his best to avoid the dryness natural to such an attempt. He inserts as much detail as his limits will permit; selects for more full description striking people and striking transactions; brings together in a single view all that relates to single topic; above all, by a regular advance of narration, never ceases to imply the regular progress of events and the steady course of time. None can deny the magnitude of such an effort. But these are merits of what is technically termed composition, and are analogous to those excellences in painting or sculpture that are more respected by artists than appreciated by the public at large.

Histories, like memoirs, are closer to art than to science, and those historians who write best will be best remembered. Gibbon is an artist who believes his words are good to eat, as well as to read, and he plainly takes pleasure in rolling them about in his mouth like sugar-plums. His fame is highest among writers, those who acutely feel and admiringly observe how difficult it would be to say so much, and leave so little untouched; to compress so many telling points; to present in so few words so apt and embracing a narrative of the whole. But the mere unsophisticated reader scarcely appreciates this; he is rather awed than delighted. The way to answer all objections to Milton is to take down the book and read him. The way to reverence Gibbon is not to read him at all, but look at him from outside, in the bookcase, and think how much there is inside; what a course of events, what a muster-roll of names, what a steady solemn sound! You will not like to take the book down, but you will think how much you could be delighted if you would.

⁂

The reader is delighted to take Macaulay's histories from the shelf. To read him for a day is to pass a day of easy thought, of pleasant placid emotion. No book is more sought after than his *History of England.* The Chancellor of the Exchequer said 'all members of Parliament had read it'. What other books could ever be fancied to have been read by them? A county member—a real county member—hardly reads two volumes per existence. Years ago Macaulay said a History of England might become more in demand at the circulating libraries than the last novel. He has actually made his words true. It is no longer a phrase of rhetoric; it is a simple fact.

But if Macaulay's *History of England* is a brilliant diorama of political pictures, it has little advantage of subject. When it appeared an honest man said, 'I suppose something happened between the years 1689 and 1697; but what happened I do not know.' Everyone knows now. No period with so little obvious interest will henceforth be so familiarly known. Macaulay has abundance; he appeals to both fancy and understanding, but only a most felicitous and rather curious genius could and would shed such a light on such a modest age. Are small men to be so largely described? Does the coarse clay of our English nature need to be represented by so fine a style of cold serenity? Should not admirable delineation be kept for admirable people? You do not want Raphael to paint sign-posts, or Palladio to build dirt-pies. The best history is but like the art of Rembrandt; it casts a vivid light on certain selected causes, and those which were best and greatest; it leaves all the rest in shadow and unseen.

Macaulay's mind is eminently gifted, but there is a want of gradation in it. He has a fine eye for probabilities, a clear perception of evidence, and makes shrewd guesses at missing links of fact; but each probability seems to him a certainty, each piece of evidence conclusive, each analogy exact. The heavy Scotch intellect is a little prone to this. One figures it as a heap of formulae, and the mathematical mill grinds with equal energy at flour perfect and imperfect—at matter which is quite certain and at matter which is only a little probable. But the great cause of this error is an abstinence from practical action. In the writings of every man of patient practicality, in the midst of whatever other defects, you will find a careful appreciation of the degrees of likelihood; a steady balancing of them one against another; a disinclination to make things too clear, to overlook the debit side of the account in mere contemplation of the enormousness of the credit. A man like Macaulay, who stands aloof from life, is not so disposed; he sits secure in his study; he loses the detective sensation.

Life is a school of probability. The data of historical narratives, especially modern histories, are a heap of confusion. No one can tell where they lie, or where they do not lie; what is in them, or what is not in them. Literature is called the 'fragment of fragments'; little has been written, and but little of that little has been preserved. So history is a vestige of vestiges. Few facts leave any trace of themselves, any witness of their occurrence; of fewer still is that witness preserved; a slight track is all anything leaves, and the confusion of life, the tumult of change, sweeps even that away in a moment. It is not possible that these data can be very fertile in certainties. Few people would make anything of them: a memoir here, a manuscript there—two letters in a magazine—an assertion by a person whose veracity is denied—these are the sort of evidence out of which a flowing narrative is to be educed. 'If you please, sir, tell me what you do *not* know' was the inquiry of a humble pupil addressed to a great man of science.

It would have been a relief to the readers of Macaulay if he had shown a little the outside of uncertainties, which there must be—the gradations of doubt, which there ought to be—the singular accumulation of difficulties, which must beset the extraction of a very easy narrative from very confused materials. Moreover, Macaulay's positiveness betrays a party spirit, as he marshals his evidence to suit his prejudices. When he inclines to a side, he inclines to it too much. His opinions are a shade too strong; his predilections some degrees at least too warm. William is too perfect, James too imperfect; the Whigs a trifle like angels, the Tories 'our inferiors'. Yet his is an honest party spirit. It does not lurk in the corners of sentences, it is not insinuated without being alleged; it does not, like the unfairness of Hume, secrete itself so subtly in the turns of the words that when you look to prove it, it is gone. On the contrary, it rushes into broad day. But as far as the effect goes, this is an error. The very earnestness of the affection leads to a reaction.

Macaulay shares in the common temperament of most historians, but he is singularly contrasted with them in one respect—he has a vivid fancy and they have a dull one. Macaulay is never dull, and it may seem hard to attempt to bring him within the scope of a theory which is so successful in explaining dullness. Yet, in a modified and peculiar form, we can perhaps find in his remarkable character unusually distinct traces of the insensibility which I ascribe to the historian. The means of scrutiny are ample. Macaulay has not spent life in a corner; if posterity should refuse to read a line of his writings, they would yet be sought out by studious inquirers, as those of a man of high political position, great notoriety, and greater oratorical power. We are not therefore obliged, as in so many cases even among contemporaries, to search for the author's character in his books alone; we are able from other sources to find out his character, and then apply it to explain the peculiarities of his works.

Macaulay has exhibited many high attainments, many dazzling talents, much singular and well-trained power. But the quality which would most strike the observers of the interior man is what may be called his *in*experiencing nature. Men of genius—Shakespeare above all among the English—are in general finer and softer than other men, distinguished by their extreme susceptibility to external experience. Every exertion of their will, every incident of their lives, influences them more deeply than it would others. Their essence is more sensitive and impressible; it receives a distinctive mark, and receives it more easily than the souls of the herd. From a peculiar sensibility, the man of genius bears the stamp of life more clearly than his fellows; even casual associations make a deep impression on him: examine his mind, and you may discern his fortunes. Macaulay has nothing of this. You could not tell what he has been. His mind shows no trace of change. What he is, he was; and what he was, he is. Macaulay early attained high development, but he has not increased it since; years have come, but they have whispered little; as was said of the second Pitt: 'He never grew, he was cast.'

Such a man would naturally think literature more instructive than life. There is a whole class of mind which prefers the literary delineation of objects to the actual sight of them. To some, life is difficult. An insensible nature, like a rough hide, resists the breath of passing things; an unobserving retina in vain depicts whatever a quicker eye does not explain. But anyone can understand a book; the work is done, the facts observed, the formulae suggested, the subjects classified. Of course it needs labour, and a following fancy, to peruse the long lucubrations and descriptions of others; but a fine detective sensibility is unnecessary; type is plain, an earnest attention will follow it and know it. To this class Macaulay

belongs, and he has characteristically maintained that dead .
authors are more fascinating than living people.

'Those friendships', Macaulay tells us,

> are exposed to no danger from the occurrences by which other
> attachments are weakened or dissolved. Time glides by; fortune
> is inconstant; tempers are soured; bonds which seem indissol-
> uble are daily sundered by interest, by emulation, or by caprice.
> But no such cause can affect the silent converse which we hold
> with the highest of human intellects. That placid intercourse is
> disturbed by no jealousies or resentments. These are the old
> friends who are never seen with new faces; who are the same in
> wealth and poverty, in glory and in obscurity. With the dead
> there is no rivalry. In the dead there is no change. Plato is never
> sullen. Cervantes is never petulant. Demosthenes never comes
> unseasonably. Dante never stays too long. No difference of
> political opinion can alienate Cicero. No heresy can excite the
> horror of Bossuet.

But Bossuet is dead; and Cicero was a Roman; and Plato
wrote in Greek. Years and manners separate us from the great.
After dinner, Demosthenes *may* come unseasonably; Dante *might*
stay too long. *We* are alienated from the politician, and have a
horror of the theologian. Dreadful idea, having Demosthenes for
an intimate friend! He had pebbles in his mouth; he was always
urging action; he spoke such good Greek; we cannot dwell on
it—it is too much. Only a mind impassive to our daily life, unalive
to bores and evils, to joys and sorrows, incapable of the deepest
sympathies, a prey to print, could imagine it. The mass of men
have stronger ties and warmer hopes. The exclusive devotion to
books tires. We require to love and hate, to act and live.

It is not unnatural that a person of Macaulay's temperament
should preserve a certain aloofness even in the busiest life. He has

been in the thick of political warfare, in the van of party conflict. Whatever a keen excitability would select for food and opportunity has been his, but he has not been excited. He has never thrown himself upon action; he has never followed trivial details with an anxious passion. He has ever been a man for a great occasion. He was by nature a *deus ex machina*. Somebody has had to fetch him. His heart was in Queen Anne's time. It may be contended that this solitary removed excellence is particularly and essentially sublime. Macaulay's *History of England* is a marvel of oratory, of eloquent entertainment. But the highest eloquence quivers with excitement; there is life-blood in the deepest action. An orator should never talk like an observatory.

CHAPTER VI

❧❧❧

Marriage and Ambition

'No one rises so high as he who knows not whither he is going,' observed Oliver Cromwell. Since leaving London I had contented myself with the rustic pleasures of Somerset and the less than onerous duties of the Bank. The year 1856 was pleasing in its fashion, as I worked by day at the bank and wrote at night in my study.

> Musings have soothed at evening hour,
> As woman's words man's world-worn power.

The year ended with an unexpected invitation. In December, the writer and mill owner W. R. Greg asked Richard Hutton if he was interested in editing *The Economist*, a journal owned by his friend the Liberal MP for Devonport and Secretary of the Treasury, James Wilson. Hutton hesitated for personal reasons, but while the offer was in abeyance, I received an invitation through the good offices of Dr Martineau, who was a friend of Greg's, to visit Claverton Manor to talk to Mr Wilson about writing some letters for *The Economist* on the impending financial crisis. As my dog cart turned up the drive to Claverton in

January 1857, I little suspected that this visit was to be the turning point of my life.

My host did not meet me upon my arrival because of a riding accident the day before, but several of his daughters greeted me in the grounds. Their liveliness reminded me of the Bennet girls in *Pride and Prejudice*, an association later confirmed when they performed a reading of the novel for my enjoyment. The eldest daughter Eliza, who was to become Elizabeth to my risible substitute for Darcy, took me down to dinner. After dinner, I accepted Mr Wilson's invitation to contribute a series of letters to *The Economist* on such topics as the Bank Charter Act. We agreed to meet again the following month in London, where the family migrated for the Parliamentary session. Mrs Wilson intimated that she would be pleased if I would pay the family a call in their house in Hertford Street—the birthplace of Lord Grey of the Reform Bill—and over the following weeks I snatched every opportunity to come under Eliza's spell.

Visits to Mayfair and Claverton were the highlights of my social life in 1857. It resulted in a courtship complete with chaperones, long walks, poetry readings and intimate letters. My mother, who was anxious for me to marry, wished me to get on with it, to which I retorted with my customary banter: 'a man's mother is his misfortune, but his wife is his fault'. Rejuvenated, I enjoyed a new life rather more vivacious than that which existed in our *ménage à trois* in Langport. In addition to the particular charms of Eliza— among them serenity and unselfishness—she and her sisters were well educated, musical, and fluent in French and German. They were without a brother; without a sister, I was delighted to be their adopted companion. What I most enjoyed about the Wilson family was their love of fun, the mixture of chaff and currency. Talks and laughter are the stuff of life, and I love to tease those whose company I most enjoy. I always tire of sense or nonsense if I am kept very continuously to either, and like my mind, which is given to jesting and irreverence, to undulate between the two as it wanders. The best charm of this earth is the medley of great things and little, of things mundane and things celestial, things low and things awful, of things eternal and things half a minute.

The cosmopolitan milieu of London which I now enjoyed at the Wilsons', little known to me as a student, was exhilarating, with a constant stream of visitors in and out: professors, financiers and statesmen. Greg and Hutton, by then editor of *The Economist*, were frequent guests. At one memorable party Tocqueville appeared after dinner, and we all changed language apart from our host, who kept to his native tongue, which he always used to great effect. Mr Wilson spent his days over his Treasury bag and his evenings in the House of Commons; yet when he finished his labours he was alive to all subjects of daily interest and ready for vigorous conversation. A tireless champion of free trade, he was a great luminary who brightened the spirits of his satellites, among whom I was then in distant orbit. But as my attentions to his daughter became apparent, I came more prominently into his purview. Our excursions took us to Kew to meet the naturalist Mr Hooker, to Millbank to see the *Great Eastern* and to the British Museum to admire the new reading room. We were ushered in to old Panizzi, who was sitting in a fine armchair with nothing to do, and he showed us some venerable fragments just in from Greece, but which I failed to admire as I prefer statues to be in one piece.

In the autumn of 1857, Eliza planned to move to Edinburgh to seek treatment for chronic headaches. As I had hopes of marriage, I felt it necessary to reveal that my mother was subject to attacks of insanity. The disclosure did not alter Eliza's feelings for me, though it did complicate her vision of the future. Soon after, I asked Mr Wilson's permission to propose to his daughter, a proposal which she accepted in the dining room in Hertford Street. I remember rushing off after breakfast to tell Hutton the news. Eliza's migration to Edinburgh a few days later meant that we were apart for several months. My letters to her during our separation show how absorbed I had become by the feelings and realities that were about to change my life. Elsewhere, my mind was mortgaged. I continued as a banker, began thinking of essays to write for the *National Review*, and set about renting and furnishing 'The Arches', our future home in Clevedon, which had beautiful views of the flat meadows below and the hazy blue hills beyond.

There twice a day the Severn fills;
  The salt sea-water passes by,
  And hushes half the babbling Wye,
And makes a silence in the hills.

Our marriage at Claverton, in April 1858, was a festive occasion, though, to much dismay, my parents were unable to attend because of my mother's incapacity. We spent our honeymoon travelling through Devonshire with a great many books, among them Matthew Arnold's poetry and the sermons of F. Denison Maurice. In a spare moment, I wrote an article on the 'Sinking Fund' for *The Economist*. Upon our return we enjoyed a round of parties and made our first trip together to Herd's Hill. I had been apprehensive about the visit but Eliza insisted on it—I sighed as a son and obeyed as a husband. The bells of All Saints pealed our arrival. The next day Eliza had to suffer the ancient custom of 'sitting up', by which she was exposed to the scrutiny of my relatives and local society. She endured the ritual with composure. My mother's vivacity and charm were on full display on this occasion, so that her mental disorder seemed more a fable than a fact. She took immediately to Eliza and her only visible eccentricity was chanting the Psalms to the butler as he cleared away the breakfast dishes.

Nothing awakens a man's ambition more than the condition of marriage, and I turned my attention to making my way in the world of letters and political economy. The association with Mr Wilson improved my prospects, while Eliza strengthened my resolve and soothed my anxious disposition. I had received favourable comment on my economic articles and praise for my literary essays. But approbation has little effect on my nerves, for I have small desire for power or renown. As my friends observe, I am prone to intellectual arrogance, possibly pride, and do not much care for general reputation. First-rate fame, the fame of great productive artists, is a matter of ultimate certainty, but no other fame is. On marrying, I was exuberant but not sanguine; my reckless cheerfulness gets on very well without the aid of hope. I can make the best of things, but have difficulty in expecting that the future will be bright. The most successful men rather over-estimate their chances of success. I cannot do this. I have always to work, like a banker, on the bare, cold probability.

As I discovered upon marriage, a bachelor is a kind of amateur in life. The affections are the best aids in what may be called the inevitable sphere of human action, and marriage is assistance in the performance of duty. Arnold says a family, or religious inter-course with the poor, is necessary for an Englishman, which I think might with pains be generalized into a complete view of the subject. Married life in Clevedon was comfortable and comforting, with frequent excursions to London, Langport and Claverton. It was arranged that I should continue to attend at the Stuckey Bank in Bristol three or four days a week and share in its management, while making regular visits to Langport and else-where in discharge of my other banking responsibilities. This gave me ample time at home to take pleasure from reading, writing and entertaining. The routine provided me with a large scene of observations, attached friends, polished acquaintance, and the tenderness of matrimonial existence. What has a light life more?

⁂

In the autumn of 1858, I produced an article on Dickens, whose writings had long fascinated me. The penetrating power of this remarkable genius among all classes at home is not inferior to its diffusive energy abroad. There is no contemporary writer whose works are read so generally through the whole house, who can give pleasure to the servants as well as to the mistress, to the children as well as to the master. No other Englishman has attained such a hold on the vast populace as Dickens; it is little, therefore, to say that he has had difficulties surmounting its attendant temptations.

Men of genius may be divided into regular and irregular. Certain minds suggest to us the ideas of symmetry and proportion. Plato's name calls up at once the impression of something measured and settled. On the other hand, writers of irregular or unsymmetrical genius are eminent either for one or some few peculiarities of mind. They have special defects on other sides of their intellectual nature; at any rate want what the scientific men of the present day would call the 'definite proportion' of faculties and qualities suited to the exact work they have in hand. The most ordinary cases of irregular genius are those in which single faculties are abnormally developed and call off the attention from all the rest of the mind by their prominence and activity. If this classification of men of genius be admitted, there can be no hesitation in assigning to Dickens his place in it. His style is an example of it. It is descriptive, racy and flowing; it is instinct with new imagery and singular illustration; but it does not indicate that due proportion of the faculties to one another which is a beauty in itself and which cannot help spreading beauty over every happy word and moulded clause.

The writings of Dickens are not those of an evenly developed or highly cultured mind; they abound in jolts and odd turns, singular twists and needless complexities. But no one can deny their great and peculiar merit. It is an odd style, the overflow of a copious mind, though not the chastened expression of an harmonious one. The novels are miscellaneous, busying themselves with the whole of human life. They aim to delineate nearly all that part of our national life which can be delineated; but you cannot read his delineation of any part without being struck with its singular incompleteness. They are like a newspaper. Everything is there, and everything is disconnected. He has pretty patches but they are graphic scraps. His shrewdness, especially in traits and small things, is wonderful. His works are full of acute remarks on petty doings and well exemplify the telling power of minute circumstantiality. But the minor species of perceptive sharpness is so different from diffused sagacity that the two scarcely ever are to be found in the same mind.

You must not ask a horse in blinkers for a large view of the landscape, and a singular defect in Dickens is his incompleteness of vision. He perpetually deals with the pecuniary part of life. Most of his characters have determined occupations, of which he is apt to talk even at too much length. But when he rises from the toiling to the luxurious classes, his genius deserts him. He knows the dry arches of London Bridge better than Belgravia. He excels in inventories of poor furniture, and is learned in pawnbrokers' tickets. But, although his creative power lives and works among the middle class and industrial section of English society, he has never painted the highest part of their daily intellectual life. His delineations of middle-class life have in consequence a harshness and meanness which do not belong to that life in reality. He omits the relieving element. He describes the figs which are sold, but not the talent which sells figs well. And it is the same want of the diffused sagacity in his own nature which has made his pictures of life so odd and disjointed, and which has deprived them of symmetry and unity.

The political opinions of Dickens have subjected him to a good deal of criticism. He has shown the desire, which is common among able and influential men, to become a political reformer. He has the ear of the public and has been quite disposed to make use of it. His politics may be described as 'sentimental radicalism', and his writings are examples both of the proper use and of the abuse of sentiment. His earlier works have excellent descriptions of the abuses which had descended to the present generation from others whose sympathy with pain was less tender. The spirit which animates Dickens shows a marked reaction to the unreformed politics of the early nineteenth century. Nothing can be better than the description of the poor debtors' gaols in *Pickwick*, or of the old parochial authorities in *Oliver Twist*. It is painful to pass from these happy instances of well-used power to the glaring abuses of the same faculty in Dickens's later books. He began by describing really removable evils in a style which would induce all persons, however insensible, to remove them if they could; he has ended by describing the natural evils and inevitable pains of the present state of being in such a manner as must tend to excite discontent and repining. He never ceases to hint that these evils are removable, though he does not say by what means.

Nothing is easier than to show the evils of anything. Dickens has often spoken, and what is worse, has taught a great number of parrot-like imitators to speak in a tone of objection to the necessary constitution of human society. If you will only write a description of it, any form of government will seem ridiculous. What is more absurd than despotism, even at its best? A king of ability or an able minister sits in an orderly room filled with memorials, returns, documents and memoranda. These are his world; among these he of necessity lives and moves. Yet how little of the real life of the nation he governs can be represented in an official form! How much real suffering is there that statistics can never tell! How much obvious good is there that no memorandum to a minister will ever mention! How much deception is there in what such documents contain! How monstrous must be the ignorance of the closet statesman, after all his life of labour, of much that a ploughman could tell him of!

A free government is almost worse. Instead of the real attention of a laborious statesman, we have now the shifting caprices of a popular assembly—elected for one object, deciding on another, shifting in its very composition; one set of men coming down to vote today, tomorrow another set, most of them eager for the dinner hour, actuated by unseen influences—by a respect for their constituents, by the dread of an attorney in a far-off borough. What people are these to control a nation's destiny, and wield the power of an empire, and regulate the happiness of millions? In either situation, we are at fault. Free government seems an absurdity and despotism is so too. Again, every form of law has a distinct expression, a rigid procedure, customary rules and forms. It is administered by human beings liable to mistake, confusion and forgetfulness, and in the long run, and on the average, is sure to be tainted with vice and fraud.

Nothing can be easier than to make a case against any particular system, by pointing out with emphatic caricature its inevitable miscarriages and by pointing out nothing else. Those who so address us may assume a tone of philanthropy, and forever exult that they are not so unfeeling as other men are. But the real tendency of their exhortations is to make men dissatisfied with their inevitable condition and, what is worse, to make them fancy that its irremediable evils *can* be remedied—by indulging in a succession of vague strivings and restless changes. Such is very much the tone with which Dickens and his followers have in later years made us familiar. To the second-hand repeaters of a cry so feeble, we can have nothing to say; if silly people cry because they think the world is silly, let them cry. But the founder of the school cannot peruse without mirth the lachrymose eloquence which his disciples have perpetrated. The soft moisture of irrelevant sentiment cannot have entirely entered into his soul. A truthful genius must have forbidden it. Let us hope that his pernicious example may incite someone of equal genius to preach with equal efficiency a sterner and wiser gospel.

My criticism of the sentimental radicalism of Dickens was a preface to an article on 'Parliamentary Reform' published in the *National Review* in January 1859, which appeared in pamphlet form the following month. It was by then impossible to suppress the forces latent in the 1832 Reform Act, which were leading to further large-scale demands with unforeseen consequences. The Act had been a success but did little to reflect the growth of urban and industrial communities. Both Whigs and Tories had pledged to do something about the franchise, but neither party had agreed a course of action. Neither Derby nor Palmerston could rule effectively and neither would give way to those who thought they could. The state of British politics was looking more like France, with the House of Commons broken into factions, which could always combine to overthrow the government. Orators require a topic. Disraeli's amusing sarcasm and Gladstone's demagogic eloquence were proof that the admirable dullness of English government in the 1850s—politics as a kind of boring business dealing with tolls and the liability of joint-stock companies—was giving way to the exhilaration of party division and the cause of the common man.

The effect of the 1832 Act had been to hide and diminish, but not to annihilate, the inequalities which had existed before. It is erroneous to argue that there should be no inequality; it should simply be distributed more usefully. The question was how to admit the working classes into a share of government without accepting the rule of mere numbers, to give them greater influence without giving them power. A real statesman should endeavour to enlarge the influence of the growing parts of the nation, as compared with the stationary parts; to augment the influence of the capitalists, but to withstand the pernicious theories which some of them advocate; to organize a means of expression for the desires of the working classes, but to withstand the commencement of a democratic revolution. Modern statesmen and modern peoples are far too willing to burden themselves with responsibilities, without verifying the principles on which action ought to proceed. All governments like to interfere; it elevates their position to make out that they can cure the evils of mankind. And all zealots wish they could interfere, for they think they can convert the rulers and manipulate state control.

There used to be much argument in favour of the democratic theory, on the ground of its supposed conformity with the abstract rights of man. This has largely passed away, but the reasons why it has been replaced are indistinct. An enthusiast may maintain, on fancied grounds of immutable morality, or from an imaginary conformity with a supernatural decree, that the ignorant should govern the instructed; but we do not comprehend how any one can maintain the proposition on grounds of expediency. The arguments from expediency, which are supposed to establish the proposition, are never set forth very clearly. We are disposed to believe, in spite of much direct assertion to the contrary, that the democratic theory still rests not so much on reason as on a kind of sentiment—on an obscure conception of abstract rights. The animation of its advocates is an indication of it. They think they are contending for the 'rights' of the people, and they endeavour to induce the people to believe so too.

It is impossible to believe that all the struggles of men for liberty—all the enthusiasm it has called forth, all the passionate emotions it has caused in the very highest minds—have their origins in calculations of advantage and a belief that such-and-such arrangements would be beneficial. The masses of men are very difficult to excite on bare grounds of self-interest; easier if a bold orator tells them confidently they are *wronged*. The foundation of government upon simple utility is but the fiction of philosophers; it has never been acceptable to the natural feelings of mankind. There is far greater truth in the formula of the French writers that *le droit dérive de la capacité*. Some sort of feeling akin to this lurks in the minds of our reformers; they think they can show that some classes now unenfranchised are as capable of properly exercising the franchise as some who have possessed it formerly, or some who have it now. The opponents of the theory are pressed with the argument that every fit person should have the franchise, and that many who are excluded are as fit as some who exercise it.

The answer to the argument is plain. Fitness to govern is not an absolute quality of any individual. That fitness is relative and comparative; it must depend on the community to be governed and on the merit of other persons who may be capable of governing that community. A savage chief may be capable of governing a savage tribe; he may have the right of governing it, for he may be the sole person capable of doing so; but he would have no right to govern England. We must also look likewise to the competitors for the sovereignty. Whatever may be your capacity for rule, you have no right to obtain the opportunity of exercising it by dethroning a person who is more capable; you are wronging the community if you do, for you are depriving it of a better government than that which you can give to it. You are wronging also the ruler you supersede, for you are depriving him of the appropriate exercise of his faculty.

The true principle is that every person has a right to so much political power as he can exercise without impeding any other person who would more fitly exercise such power. If we apply this to the lower classes of society we see the reason why, notwithstanding their numbers, they must be comparatively less influential. There are individual exceptions, but in questions of this magnitude it may be said that political intelligence will in general exist in the well educated rather than in the poorly educated. Whatever their capacity may be, it must be less in the lower than the higher classes, whose occupations are more instructive and whose education is more prolonged. Any measure for enfranchising the lower classes that would overpower, and consequently disfranchise, the higher should be resisted on the ground of 'abstract right'. It would simply take power from those who have the superior capacity and vest it in those who have but an inferior capacity. If we probe the subject to the bottom, we shall find that justice is on the side of a graduated rule, in which all persons should have an influence proportioned to their political capacity, and it is at this graduation that the true maxims of representative government really aim.

By the operation of a truly democratic Constitution, the selection of rulers is submitted to the direct vote of the populace. The lower classes are then told that they are perfectly able to judge. Demagogues assert it to them without ceasing, for all selfish ambition gravitates towards the demos. The Constitution itself is appealed to as an incontrovertible witness to the fact. Since it has placed the supreme power in the hands of the lower and more numerous classes, it would be contravening it to suppose that the real superiority was in the higher and fewer. In consequence, history teaches that under a democratic government those who reflect the feelings of the majority have a greater chance of being chosen to rule. The natural effect of such a government is to mislead the poor. There is a risk of vulgarizing the whole tone, method and conduct of our political institutions and public business. One can see how completely this has happened in America, a country far more fitted for the democratic experiment than any old country can be.

The coarsening of political life is not a mere external expression, for it eats away the ability of a nation. A vulgarity in the tone of discussion disgusts cultivated minds with the subject of politics; they will not apply themselves to master a topic, which, besides its natural difficulties, is encumbered with disgusting phrases, low arguments, and the undisguised language of coarse selfishness. A high morality shrinks with the shyness of superiority from intruding itself into the presence of low debates. The inevitable consequence of vulgarizing Parliament would be the deterioration of public opinion in its more refined elements. The characteristic danger for great nations, like the Romans or the English, which have a long history of continuous creation, is that they may at last fail from the weakening of the great institutions which they have created.

CHAPTER VII

※2◎☆

London and *The Economist*

M Y pamphlet on reform thrust me into the inner circle of political life in the capital. My father-in-law wrote to me saying how everyone spoke of it in glowing terms. Thackeray asked the publisher to supply him with this 'wonderfully clever pamphlet'. Robert Lowe, then Vice-President of the Committee of the Council on Education, said it was the best thing he had read on the subject, though its practical recommendations on the franchise were too refined for popular consumption and impossible to implement. As it happened, the House of Commons remained in a state of confusion about the franchise. Whilst I was noticed as a political philosopher, there was little hope of passing my modest proposals, which included the transfer of a moderate number of seats to towns with a high industrial population. Nothing is so easy as to be sensible on paper. A Clerk of the Treasury said that my ideas were so sensible that they would please no one.

I derived great advantage from my conversations with my father-in-law, and an affectionate intimacy grew up between us. He had an unusually generous and balanced mind, with the added excitement of origination, and he kindly indulged my impulse to extend myself into the world of affairs. We both had an experiencing nature, and contact with him revived my youthful cheerfulness and put the world of national politics within reach. He invited those who had expressed an admiration for my pamphlet on Parliamentary reform to join us for dinner at his new residence in Upper Belgrave Street. One could not have had brought together a finer collection of political animals than, among others, Lord Grey, Lord Granville, Gladstone and Thackeray, men on both sides of the question of changes to the Constitution. The novelty of a dinner party on a division night proved a success and several others followed.

Such events provided freshness, but I was always happy to return home to Clevedon, where I was known as a provincial banker rather than a pamphleteer among the political magnates. The to and fro between city and countryside, banking and literature, kept me from the doldrums to which I am prone. I had reached a place, at once mobile and settled, in which I had received the inestimable permission to be myself. I lived something of a double life, which lent perspective. I dined with cabinet ministers who knew nothing of my pack of harriers, and hunted with country gentlemen who had no idea that I had written on Shakespeare and Parliamentary reform. My own father was largely ignorant of my life beyond the Stuckey Bank. In London I was taken up as a man to watch, but I lived my life in Somerset as an ordinary species, without cheers from the gallery, which provided my growing ambition with a corrective scepticism.

Early in 1860, Gladstone had delivered his great budget speech, a very different one from that which he was expected to deliver. We had enjoyed our conversation over dinner at the Wilsons', which led to a correspondence on financial policy and invitations from Gladstone to breakfasts at Carlton House Terrace. Despite our cordial relations, I felt that essayists in the quarterlies had a peculiar mission in relation to the characters of public men. I believe it is their duty to be personal and critical. The names of public men are forever on our lips, to the extent that we never take up a newspaper without seeing them. But this incessant treatment of personality is fragmentary; it is composed of chance criticism of special traits, of fugitive remarks on temporary measures, of casual praise and casual blame. We can expect little else from what is written in haste. Public men must bear this criticism as they can. Those whose names are perpetually in men's mouths must not be pained if singular things are sometimes said of them. Still *some* deliberate truth should be spoken of our statesmen, and if essayists do not speak it, who will? Consequently, I turned my mind to Gladstone in the *National Review*.

In 1860, I believed Gladstone to be a man of great gifts whose political future was uncertain. He was then in transition from Toryism to Liberalism and was a mystery to both the country at large and his colleagues. He was thus a 'problem'. Who could tell whether he would be the greatest orator of a great administration and rule the House of Commons, or would aid in destroying many ministries and share in none? His peculiarities were not so unaccountable as they seemed. As an old Whig who did not approve of his discussion on the Budget once muttered: 'Ah, Oxford on the surface, but Liverpool below', a revealing line that will long be remembered, though not in the splenetic sense in which it was intended. Gladstone does combine, in a very curious way, many of the characteristics which we generally associate with the place of his education and many of those which we usually connect with the place of his birth. Underneath the scholastic polish of an Oxford education, he has the speculative hardihood, the eager industry of a Lancashire merchant.

Gladstone has what may be called oratorical and didactic impulses, with a schoolman's taste for contentious hair-splitting. He has the courage of his ideas and will convince his audience and in the process convince himself. He has, as Coleridge might have said, *a nature* towards his audience. He is sure, if they only knew what he knows, that they would feel as he feels, and believe as he believes. He longs to pour forth his own belief; he cannot rest till he has contradicted everyone else. And by this he conquers. This living faith, this enthusiasm, this confidence, call it what you will, is an extreme power in human affairs. In the composition of an orator, the hope, the credulous hope, that he will convince his audience is the primitive incentive which is the spring of his influence and the source of his power. Gladstone has—and it is one of the springs of great power—a real faith in the higher parts of human nature; he believes, with all his heart and soul and strength, that there is such a thing as truth. He has the soul of a martyr with the intellect of an advocate.

These great faculties give Gladstone an extraordinary influence in English politics. England is a country governed by labour and by speech. Gladstone will work and can speak, and the result is what we see. With a flowing eloquence and a lofty heroism, with an acute intellect and endless knowledge; with courage to conceive large schemes, and a voice which will persuade men to adopt those schemes—it is not singular that he is of himself a power in Parliamentary life. He can do there what no one else living can do. But the effect of these peculiar faculties is by no means entirely favourable. In almost every one of them some faulty tendency is latent, which may produce bad effects—in Gladstone's case has often done so. The oratorical impulse is a disorganizing impulse and is damaging to the exercise of the imagination. The higher faculties of the mind require a certain calm, and the excitement of oratory is injurious to that calm. Placid moderation is necessary to coherent success. The disorganizing effects of his greatest peculiarities have played a principal part in shaping Gladstone's character and course. By 1860, they had annoyed the old Whigs, confounded the country gentlemen, and puzzled the nation generally.

A constitutional statesman in the present day lives by following public opinion. He may profess to guide it a little; he may hope to modify it in detail; he may help to exaggerate and to develop it, but he hardly hopes for more. And what does this mean except that such a statesman has to follow the varying currents of a varying world; to adapt his public expressions, if not his private belief, to the tendencies of the hour; to be in no slight measure the slave—the petted and applauded slave, but still the slave—of the world which he seems to rule? Nor is this all. A minister is not simply the servant of the public; he is also the advocate of his colleagues. Indeed, the life of a great minister is the life of a great advocate. Parliamentary life rarely admits the autocratic supremacy of an original intellect; the times were singularly unfavourable to it, and Gladstone was the last man to obtain it.

No political life could be imagined which was worse for a mind like Gladstone's. He is naturally prone to vehement arguments. But he has followed a career in which it is necessary to follow a changing guide and to obey a fluctuating opinion; to argue vehemently for tenets which you dislike; to defend a given law today, to propose repealing the same law tomorrow. Accumulated experience shows that the public life of our Parliamentary statesmen is singularly unsteadying, is painfully destructive of coherent principle. We may easily conceive how dangerous it must be to a mind like Gladstone's, which, by its intrinsic nature, is impetuous. In 1860, his future was unpredictable, for he needed to learn the creed of his time as he could not impose his own. The vehement orator, the impulsive thinker, is the last man from whom we should expect an original policy. Gladstone was the expositor of his generation, the advocate of its conclusions, the admired orator in whom all could take pride. But would he become more?

The recent past has been an age of destruction. The measures by which it will be remembered—the repeal of the Corn Laws and Catholic disabilities—were abolitions. When I wrote my essay on Gladstone, the country had reached the term of the destructive period. We could not abolish all our laws for there were few remaining with which educated men found fault. The questions which remained were questions of construction; how the lower classes were to be admitted to a share of political power without absorbing the whole power; how the natural union of Church and State was to be adapted to an age of divided religious opinion. These, and such as these, were becoming the topics of our home policy.

Destruction is easy; construction is very difficult. Progressive governments like to proceed with ambitious plans, which often carry them away from thoughtful intentions. A constitutional statesman—Peel is perhaps our greatest exemplar—is a man of common opinions and uncommon abilities, who understands our real public opinion. He will have to disregard loud agitators; will not yield to a loud voice, but listen for a still small voice; will have to seek for the opinion which is treasured in secret rather than for that which is noised abroad. I ventured to say that if Gladstone would accept the conditions of his age; if he would guide himself by the mature, settled and cultured reflection of his time, and not by its loud and noisy organs—he would leave a great name, be useful to his country, and might steady and balance his own mind.

※

Such was my estimate of Gladstone in the summer of 1860, which he took in generous spirit, saying it was true in the parts least favourable to his vanity. It had been written in the tranquillity of Clevedon. But our lives there were about to change irrevocably. In the autumn of 1859, Mr Wilson had set sail for India as the Finance Member of the Viceroy's Council and Chancellor of the Indian Exchequer, a five-year appointment which entailed great personal sacrifices on his part. He had been asked to deal with the economic chaos that the Mutiny had left in its wake, a task he was taking in his stride with a new Indian budget. We corresponded at length on Indian affairs, and in July 1860 he wrote his last letter to me, in which he complained of the onerous work and an attack of dysentery contracted in the hot, damp climate of Calcutta. Within weeks he was dead. For a month we were unconscious of our loss. The official notice from the Governor-General had been delayed, and we had been pursuing our usual activities at 'The Arches', when my sister-in-law Julia read of her father's death in *The Times*. I shall never forget the cries and confusion of voices in my study where we gathered, and then silence, as if all time had stopped.

I suffered greatly from Mr Wilson's death; more than I could have supposed possible. I had such extreme pleasure in talking to him on his favourite subjects before he went to India and, after he went away, from writing on the same subjects in *The Economist* where he used to write. Since our first meeting, I had formed the habit of referring to his mind and keeping up a sort of mental dialogue with him. A consummate judge of administrative affairs, he had the energy and masculine activity that are necessary for social action. His conversation was always animated and heartening; he had, as Hutton said, a thorough enjoyment of all the more genial sides of life. He had never known periods of apathy and concentrated on those issues which he thought most important, on which he could form a settled principle, which spared him from the lethargy that often results from scepticism. To the last hour of his life he was always sanguine. His tendency was to look at everything in a bright and cheerful aspect and to form a somewhat too favourable judgment of things and men. One proof of this may be sufficient—he was five years Secretary to the Treasury and did not leave it a suspicious man.

During his absence, Mr Wilson had left me in general charge of *The Economist*, with Hutton as editor. On his death, I was appointed an executor of his estate along with his brothers. His affairs had to be settled and *The Economist* directed. Suddenly, his widow and daughters found themselves its proprietors. Within a year Eliza and I moved from Clevedon to the Wilson home in Upper Belgrave Street. I resigned the local management of the Stuckey Bank in Bristol to undertake the supervision of the London office. Privately, the government sounded me out about replacing Mr Wilson as the Finance Member for India. Though flattered, I decided not to pursue the possibility because of family obligations and because I had not the range of experience to deal with the burdens of the office.

Such precipitous changes were not entirely to our liking. The work was invigorating, but leaving the countryside and calm of Clevedon was a hardship. The bustle of the capital is not without appeal, but most of those who make up London society lack the charm of genial light-heartedness. Indeed, a great part of the 'best' English people keep their mind in a state of decorous dullness. They maintain their dignity; they get obeyed; they are good and charitable to their dependants. But they have no notion of *play* of mind, no conception that the charm of society depends on it. They think cleverness an antic, and have a constant though needless horror of being thought to have any of it. So much does this stiff dignity give the tone, that the few Englishmen capable of social brilliancy mostly secrete it. They reserve it for persons whom they can trust, and whom they know to be capable of appreciating its *nuances*.

I delight in discussing anything but business with intimate friends; but life in the capital requires a greater degree of social energy and ambition than I possess. It is inconceivable to me that enjoyment is to be found in meeting so many new people. Those you speak to become an intellectual burden because you may see them again, and you must be able to recognize and be willing to converse with them. One regrets having to bore the person one is speaking to because the situation in which one finds oneself allows of nothing better. At conventional London dinners one talks nothing but nonsense. In polite society a gentleman is expected never to speak to women on serious issues with any wit or subtlety; between two pillars of crinoline, you eat and are resigned. Reserve is my defence. A managed reticence has often spared me from trivial conversations and quelled misguided ambitions. I conceal my tendency to playful provocations behind a mask of formality and console myself that humour gains from constant suppression. There is an innocent pleasure in being misunderstood.

≈⊚≈

Under the terms of the agreement drawn up by Mr Wilson's trustees, I became the custodian of *The Economist*. By the time I became the paper's editor in the summer of 1861, Hutton had moved a few doors down the Strand to revitalize the *Spectator*. My intention was to shape *The Economist* in keeping with Mr Wilson's financial views and business-like method. Our circulation was modest. We wished to give our readers what they wanted and did not seek to compete with the dailies and their detailed coverage of politics, or the quarterlies and their extended literary articles. Money-making, the trade cycle, and the methods of business were staples. Our typical reader is a businessman, banker or trader, who prefers statistics to abstractions and has little patience for padding. He is generally cool, with his own business to attend to, and has a set of ordinary opinions arising from and suited to ordinary life. He does not desire an article that is too profound, but one which he can lay down and say, 'an excellent article, very excellent, exactly my own sentiments'. A grave man on the Coal Exchange does not wish to be an apostle of novelties among the contemporaneous dealers in fuel.

Over the last fifteen years, I have written innumerable articles for *The Economist*, which has been a test of stamina if not originality. Everyone who has written for more than one news-paper knows how his style catches the tone of each paper while he is writing for it. But no one can think to much purpose when he is studying to write in a style not his own. Thus I did not set myself to copy the traditional style to which the readers of the paper were familiar. As in my literary essays, I aimed to be animated and conversational, but brevity is at a premium when talking about money to non-literary readers. An editor should be a trustee for the subscribers. In my articles for *The Economist* I have always had the conventional City man in my mind's eye, a man unskilled in literature and turning phrases, with a limited vocabulary and little knowledge of theory.

In journalism, as in politics, it is often braver to have few opinions than opinions on everything. There is pressure to have a view, but the habit of always advancing a view commonly destroys the capacity for holding one. The laxity of principle imputed to old politicians is, by the time they are old, as much intellectual as moral. They have argued on all sides of everything, till they can believe on no side of anything and are dispossessed of ideas. A characteristic of the same sort has been observed in journalism. Out of a million articles that everybody has read in the papers, can any one person trace a single marked idea to a single article? One of our most celebrated contemporaries was asked his opinion on ten great subjects in succession, and on its appearing that he had no opinions, he said, apologetically, 'You see, ma'am, I have written for *The Times.*' Opinion is cheap, information dear; at *The Economist* we try to strike a profitable balance between the two.

Just as I do not enjoy discussing business with friends, I do not wish to dwell on the commercial issues which took up much of my time at *The Economist*. Banking and the silver trade are topics fit for men of business but have little appeal to the literary public. Just as one cannot like a Calvinistic divine when we see him in the pulpit, it is tiresome to read about the currency even when it concerns the bank-notes which we use. The world of commerce is essential to human progress. But the contrast between the nature of the human mind and its employments is absurd. As Goldsmith says, 'honour sinks where commerce long prevails'. In the old world at least, we are basely subjected to the yoke of coin. How can a merchant be a soul? What relation to an immortal being has the price of linseed or the brokerage on hemp? Can an undying creature debit petty expenses and charge for carriage paid? The soul ties its shoes; the mind washes its hands in a basin. All is incongruous.

One commercial issue—shareholding—does widely translate to the wider public; those with money think of increasing it. As a rule, those who hunger after riches will have riches, and those who hunger not will not. Still, those who hunger need the nourishment of sound financial advice. Under Mr Wilson, *The Economist* had hated humbug and took a stern view of investment. Over the years, I have tried to introduce some common sense on financial matters. Common sense teaches that booksellers should not speculate in hops or bankers in turpentine; that savings should not be hazarded because they may yield much; that families may be ruined by rashness, and children made beggars by an investment without information. *The Economist* advised investors to use their common sense and avoid the enticements of ingenious speculators, who are florid on out of the way obligations which they can't manage, but often fail to manage appropriately those which they do manage.

The history of the trade cycle had taught me that a period of a low rate of return on investment inexorably leads towards irresponsible investment. In financial affairs, as elsewhere, men rarely desire what they already have. An over-confidence in times of modest prosperity leads John Bull, irritated by 2 per cent, into reckless investment. People won't take 2 per cent and cannot bear a loss of income. Instead, they invest their careful savings in something impossible—a canal to Kamchatka, a railway to Watchet, a plan for animating the Dead Sea. We can only hope that capitalists will exercise a discretion—that merchants will not over-trade—that shopkeepers will not over-stock—that the non-mercantile public will bear a reduction in income—that they will efface superfluities, endure adversity, and abolish champagne. But unless self-denial is exercised and common sense exerted the case is hopeless. One of two alternatives must be taken. If the old and tried and safe investments no longer yield their accustomed returns, we must take what they do yield, or try what is untried. We must either be poorer or less safe, less opulent or less secure.

Commerce tends to give much to those who have much, and from such as have little takes away that little. But in the interest of security and common sense, *The Economist* distilled the primitive considerations of investment, which conformed to my own propensity to prudence in personal finance. First, whose labour do you propose to get a share of? Secondly, what is your certainty that you will get a share in it? The paper's advice to investors, who are acquisitive but often innocent in matters of finance, has been consistent: have nothing to do with anything unless you understand it, divide your investments, and be wary of taking advice from others. It is right to take counsel and to use it as a ground for a decision, but it must be used to aid the intellect, not to supersede the discretion. Most advisors counsel what is safe for themselves, but then they suppose a competency which probably the person advised does not possess.

In commerce, as elsewhere, the same disposition to excessive action is very apparent to careful observers. Part of every mania is caused by the impossibility of getting people to confine themselves to the amount of business for which their capital is sufficient, and in which they can engage safely. In some degree, this is caused by the wish to get rich; but in a considerable degree, too, by the mere love of activity. There is a greater propensity to action in such men than they have the means of gratifying. Operations with their own capital will only occupy four hours of the day, and they wish to be industrious for eight hours, and so they are ruined. If they could only have sat idle the other four hours, they would have been rich. The immense energy and activity which have given us our place in the world have in many cases descended to those who do not find in modern life any mode of using that activity, and of venting that energy.

At a time when we are all somewhat disposed to blame commercial men for what we call their speculative indiscretions, people are apt to forget how much excuse there is in the high development which modern commerce has assumed, for the sort of restless activity which is almost certain to result in indiscretions. Political economy has to a certain extent misled literary men—and, therefore, popular opinion, which of course takes its tone very much from what the newspapers say—as to the kind of faculty needed in commerce. The qualities required in the higher departments of commerce are very rare, very remarkable, and of a very narrow kind. They are to the qualities required in the lower departments very much what the qualities needed by a great strategist, who has to handle large armies, are to the qualities needed by a soldier, who has nothing more to do than go through with his own little task of obedience to orders.

Commerce is like war: its result is patent. Do you make money or do you not make it? There is as little appeal from figures as from battles. The capitalist is the general of the army, the motive power in modern production. He fixes on the plan of operations, organizes its means, and superintends its execution. If he does this well, the business succeeds and continues; if he does it ill, the business fails and ceases. Everything depends on the correctness of the unseen decisions, on the secret sagacity of the determining mind. And I am careful to dwell on this, though it is so obvious, and though no man of business would think it worth mentioning, because the books forget it—because the writers of books are not familiar with it. They are taken with the conspicuousness of the working classes; they hear them say, it is we who made Birmingham, we who made Manchester. But you might as well say that it was the compositors who made *The Times* newspaper. No doubt the craftsmen were necessary, but of themselves they were insufficient.

We often talk as if the haste to be rich, the mere desire of wealth, were the only motive power in these great speculative transactions which, when they fail, cause so much misery and so much scandal. But no mistake could be greater. We do not for a moment mean that the desire to be rich, the passion for making wealth, is not far too great—and in a considerable measure the cause of the speculative rashness we see. But it is not by any means the sole cause. There is greediness and avarice enough in the City, but, probably, hardly more than in the West End. The chief difference is that in the City such greediness as there is enters so completely into the chief work of life that no man can really tell where it is that his intellectual interest in his work ends, and his craving for wealth begins.

By far the best check on this intense vitality and recklessness of the commercial intelligence would result from such wider culture as would give these men other keen intellectual interests as well as those which are identified with their occupations. It is not the widely cultivated men who are the most eager in their commercial enterprises. They have other channels for their intellectual life and energy, and accordingly they can afford to limit the energy of their commercial enterprise within the bounds of prudence. It is the men who have no other intellectual life except the life of commercial enterprise who are the truly dangerous men—not dangerous because they are generally less scrupulous, but because they are more eager for the full employment of their powers than their better-educated contemporaries. The energy of commerce runs with a strong current, in part because it runs between such very narrow banks. Let it find a number of different mouths, a delta instead of a single opening, and it will not rush on with the same dangerous velocity. Culture always diminishes intensity. And in the commercial world we could well afford to favour that result.

CHAPTER VIII

Spare Mind

EDITING *The Economist* turned my attention increasingly to commercial issues, but my spare mind always looks to intellectual pursuits for relief. The same suspicion of abstract speculations in commerce has made me suspicious of philosophical speculations, which bear the same traces of excessive impulse. Ideologies can be dangerous things. Great and terrible systems of divinity and philosophy lie round about us, which, if true, might drive a wise man mad. Every sort of philosophy has been systematized, and yet as these philosophies utterly contradict one another, most of them cannot be true. Unproved abstract principles without number have been eagerly caught up by sanguine men, and then carefully spun out into books and theories, which were to explain the whole world. The mass of a system attracts the young and impresses the unwary; but cultivated people are very dubious about it. Fortunately, most people are too well balanced—or too stupid—to be seriously affected by it. They are ready to receive hints and suggestions, and the smallest real truth is very welcome. But large books of deductive philosophy are much to be suspected, for they are likely to contain a strange mixture of truth and error. The superfluous energy of mankind has flowed over into philosophy and religion, and has worked into big systems what should have been left as little suggestions.

Given my aversion to abstract doctrines, I prefer to turn my mind to history, biography and literature, which offer greater insight into character and truths on a human scale. The appearance of Earl Stanhope's *Life of William Pitt* in 1861—a book of good sense and languid accuracy—prompted an essay in the *National Review* on a Prime Minister who remains subject to misunderstanding. He had never had even a decent biographer, though the peculiarities of his career are singularly inviting to literary ambition. Pitt appealed to me as a great man with a robust sense of fun, which he disguised from the vulgar by a rigid mask of grave dignity. His life had much of the solid usefulness of modern times, and not a little also of the romance of old times. He was skilled in economical reform, but retained some of the majesty of old-world eloquence. He was as keen in small figures as a rising politician now; yet he was a despotic premier at an age when, in these times, a politician can barely aspire to be an under-secretary.

Pitt came to power with a fresh mind. And not only so; he came to power with the cultivated thought of a new generation— the first statesman to learn from Adam Smith and apply the principles of free trade against the accumulation of irritable and stupid prejudice. Too many of us scarcely remember how young a man he was. He was born in 1759, and might well have been in his vigour in 1830. He governed men of the generation before him. Alone among English statesmen, while yet a youth he was governing middle-aged men. He had the power of applying the eager thought of five-and-twenty, of making it rule over the petty knowledge and trained acquiescence of five-and-fifty. Alone as yet, and alone perhaps for ever in our Parliamentary history, while his own mind was still original, while his own spirit was still unbroken, he was able to impose an absolute yoke on acquiescent spirits whom the world had broken for him.

Pitt was by no means an excited visionary. He had by no means one of those minds upon which great ideas fasten as a fanaticism. There was among his contemporaries a great man, who was in the highest gifts of abstract genius, in the best acquisitions of political culture, far superior to him. But in the mind of Burke, great ideas were a supernatural burden, a superincumbent inspiration. He saw a great truth and he saw nothing else. At all times with the intense irritability of genius, in later years with the extreme one-sidedness of insanity, he was content, in season and out of season, with the great visions which had been revealed to him, with the great lessons which he had to teach, and which he could but very rarely induce any one to hear.

The mind of Pitt was an absolute contrast to this. He had extreme discretion, tested at the most trying conjunctures. In 1784, when he had no power, when there was a hostile majority in the House of Commons, when he had no sure majority in the House of Lords, he guided the most feeble administration of modern times so ably and so dexterously that in a few months it became the strongest. A mind with so delicate a tact as this is entitled to some merit for adhering to distant principles. It is this singular discretion which is Pitt's peculiar merit, because it belongs to a class of statesmen who are most apt to be defective in that discretion. He was an oratorical statesman, and an oratorical statesman means an excitable statesman. How is the exercise of this oratorical art to be reconciled with terrestrial discretion? Is it possible that the same mind which can touch the hearts of all men can also be alive to the petty interests of itself? A dry man can do the necessary business; an excitable man can give to the popular house of Parliament the necessary excitement. Finding the microscopic power and the telescopic power in one statesman is the perpetual difficulty. Pitt, with surpassing ability and surpassing ease, combined the two; scarcely anyone else has done so.

Mankind judges a great statesman principally by the most marked and memorable passage in his career. The event in Pitt's life most deeply implanted in the popular memory is his resistance to the French Revolution, a time of monumental crisis in European and English affairs. It is his handling of this crisis that has made him the object of affection to extreme Tories, and of suspicion to reasonable Liberals. Yet no suspicion was ever more unfounded and false. It can be proved that, in all the other parts of Pitt's life, the natural tendency of his favourite plan was uniformly Liberal. Under his auspices, the spirit of legislative improvement which characterises modern times may almost be said to begin. At the time of the French Revolution he only did what the immense majority of the English people deliberately desired. He did it anxiously, with many misgivings, and in opposition to his natural inclinations. It is very dubious whether, given the temper of the French nation and the temper of the English nation, a war between them could have been avoided.

There are two kinds of statesmen to whom, at different times, representative government gives an opportunity and a career—dictators and administrators. There are certain men—Lincoln most notably in our time—who are called in conjunctures of great danger to save the state. When national peril was imminent, all nations have felt it needful to select the best man who could be found—for better, for worse; to put unlimited trust in him; to allow him to do whatever he wished, and to leave undone whatever he did not approve of. The qualities which are necessary for a dictator are two—a commanding character and an original intellect. All other qualities are secondary. If he has force of character to overawe men into trusting him, and originality of intellect sufficient to enable him to cope with the pressing, terrible and critical events with which he is selected to cope, it is enough.

Every subordinate shortcoming, every incidental defect, will be pardoned. 'Save us!' is the cry of the moment; in the confident hope of safety, any deficiency will be overlooked, and any frailty pardoned.

The genius required for a great administrator is not so imposing. Ordinary administrators are very common; everyday life requires and produces everyday persons. But a really great administrator thinks not only of the day but of the morrow. He does not only what he must but what he wants, is eager to extirpate every abuse, and on the watch for every improvement. He is on a level with the highest political thought of his time, and persuades his age to be ruled according to it. Administration in this large sense includes legislation, for it is concerned with the far-seeing regulation of future conduct, as well as with the limited management of the present. Great dictators are doubtless rare in political history, but they are not more so than great administrators. It is not easy to manage any age; it is not easy to be on a level with the highest thought of any age; but to manage that age according to that highest thought is among the most arduous tasks of the world. The intellectual character of a dictator is noble and simple; that of a great administrator and legislator is also complex.

Pitt had in the most complete perfection the faculties of a great administrator, and he added to it the commanding temperament, though not the creative intellect, of a great dictator. He was tried by long and prosperous years, which exercised to the utmost his peculiar faculties. He was tried likewise by a terrible crisis, which he did not understand as we understand it now, but in which he showed a hardihood of resolution and a consistency of action which captivated the English people. The characteristic merit of Pitt is that in the midst of harassing details, in the midst of obvious cares, in the face of most keen, most able and most stimulated opposition, he applied his whole power to the accomplishment of great but practicable schemes. He had some success in addressing the chaos of our financial and economic legislation and, had not the strong counteracting influence of the French Revolution changed the national opinion, he would unquestionably have amended our Parliamentary representation.

The crisis which the French Revolution presented to an English statesman was one rather for a great dictator than for a great administrator. Undoubtedly, Pitt did not comprehend the Revolution in France. He overrated the danger of a revolution in this country; he entirely over-estimated the power of the democratic assailants, and he entirely under-estimated the force of the conservative, maintaining, restraining, and reactionary influence. But it is not given to many men to conquer such difficulties; it is not given to the greatest of administrators to apprehend entirely new phenomena. A highly imaginative statesman, a man of great moments and great visions, a greater Lord Chatham, might have done so, but the educated sense and equable dexterity of Pitt failed. He showed most distinctly how potent is the influence of a commanding character just when he most exhibited the characteristic limitation of even the best administrative intellect.

⁂

Life at Upper Belgrave Street was agreeable, but the intense sociability of the family—'At Homes', luncheons, dinners, balls, the opera and theatre—tested my stamina. I enjoy the social and cultural life of the capital as long as I am not responsible for the arrangements and can join or not, as I feel inclined. I was the solitary man in a house of spirited women. The romances of my sisters-in-law were a recurring domestic theme; books, I submitted, were a healing balm. There were daily rides in the park with my wife in our phaeton, and Sunday visits to my Aunt and Uncle Reynolds in Hampstead. Every fortnight I returned to Langport, to attend meetings of the Stuckey Bank and to see my parents. On occasion, I stayed with my friends Sir Arthur and Lady Elton at Clevedon Court, and with the historian Freeman, who had a house near Wells. Given my hectic life among the sombre men of politics and the City, the companionship of old friends and early associations has been essential to my contentment.

Since our days together at University College, I had enjoyed the intellectual company of Clough, and his premature death of malaria in Florence in November 1861 was a dreadful shock to all his friends. The publication of an edition of his poems the following year was an opportunity to offer an opinion on his life and writing. His poetry depicts an intellect in a state which is natural to man in the present world. He was a man of strong and clear intellect, who had a fatigued, world-weary way of looking at great subjects. The flavour of his mind disinclined him to overrate the doings of his friends and compelled him to underrate his own writings and capabilities. He could not have borne to have his poems reviewed with 'nice remarks' and sentimental epithets. To offer petty praise and posthumous compliments to an ascetic of his taciturn temper would have been like buying sugar-plums for St Simon Stylites.

There are two great opinions about everything. There are two about the universe itself, which Kant taught us to see as formed of distinct spheres of experience. There is the vast, visible, indisputable, material world, of which we never lose consciousness, of which no one seriously denies the existence. On the other hand, there is the invisible, spiritual world, about which men are not agreed at all, which all but a few admit to exist somehow and somewhere, but as to the nature or locality of which there is not efficient popular demonstration. But the nobler we conceive the unseen world which is in us and about us, in which we live and move, the more unlike that world becomes to the world which we *do* see.

Two opinions as to the universe naturally result from this fundamental contrast of the visible and invisible. There are minds like Voltaire who have no sense of the invisible world whatever, who have no ear for religion, who are in the technical sense unconverted. They are, as a rule, acute, sensible, discerning and humane; but the first observation which the most ordinary person would make about them is that they are 'limited'. On the other hand, there are those whose minds have not only been converted, but are in some sense *inverted*. They are so occupied with the invisible world as to be absorbed in it entirely; they have no true conception of that which stands plainly before them; they are wrapt up in their own faith in an unseen existence. They rush upon mankind with 'Ah, there it is! There it is!—don't you see it?' and so incur the ridicule of the age.

The best of us try to avoid both fates. We strive to make the most of both worlds. We know the invisible world cannot be duly discerned, or perfectly appreciated. We know that we see as in a glass darkly, but still we look on the glass. We frame to ourselves some image which we know to be incomplete, which probably is in part untrue, which we try to improve day by day, the defects of which we do not deny, but which we hope, when the accounts are taken, may be found not utterly unlike the unknown reality. This is, it seems, the most sensible religion for finite beings living on the very edge of two dissimilar worlds, on the very line on which the infinite, unfathomable sea surges up, and just where the queer little bay of this world ends. We count the pebbles on the shore, and image to ourselves as best we may the secrets of the deep.

There are, however, some minds, and Clough's was among them, which will not accept what appears to be an intellectual destiny. They swim against the tide, struggle against the limitations of mortality, and will not condescend to use the natural and

needful aids of human thought. As flawed beings they scarcely
can hope to attain an 'Actual Abstract'. They feel, and they rightly
feel, that every image, every translation, every mode of conception by which the human mind tries to place before itself the
Divine mind, is imperfect, halting, changing. They feel, from
their own experience, that there is no one such mode of representation which will suit their own minds at all times, and they smile
with bitterness at the notion that they could contrive an image
which will suit all other minds. They could not become fanatics
or missionaries, or even common preachers, without forfeiting
their natural dignity and forgoing their very essence. If you offer
them any religion, they won't have that; if you offer them no religion, they will not have that either; if you ask them to accept a
new and as yet unrecognised religion, they altogether refuse to do
so. Clough has expressed what may be called their essential
religion:

> O Thou whose image in the shrine
> Of human spirits dwells divine;
> Which from that precinct once conveyed,
> To be to outer day displayed,
> Doth vanish, part, and leave behind
> Mere blank and void of empty mind,
> Which wilful fancy seeks in vain
> With casual hopes to fill again!
> O Thou, that in our bosom's shrine
> Dost dwell, unknown because divine!
> I thought to speak, I thought to say,
> 'The light is here,' 'Behold the way,'
> 'The voice was thus,' and 'thus the word,'
> And, 'thus I saw,' and 'that I heard,'—
> But from the lips that half essayed
> The imperfect utterance fell unmade.

O Thou, in that mysterious shrine
Enthroned, as I must say, divine!
I will not frame one thought of what
Thou mayest either be or not.
I will not prate of 'thus' and 'so,'
An be profane with 'yes' and 'no,'
Enough that in our soul and heart
Thou, whatso'er Thou may'st be, art.

It was natural that Clough should incline to some such creed as this. He had by nature an exceedingly real mind, in the good sense of that expression. The actual visible world as it was, and as he saw it, exercised over him a compulsory influence. The hills among which he had wandered, the cities he had visited, the friends whom he knew—these were his world. Many minds of the poetic sort easily melt down these palpable facts into some impalpable ether of their own. But to him, the vulgar, outward world was a primitive fact. Reconcile what you have to say with green peas, for green peas are certain; such was Clough's idea. He had a straining, inquisitive, critical mind; he scrutinised every idea before he took it in; he did not allow the moral forces of life to act as they should; he was content to gain a belief 'by going on living'. He felt the coarse facts of the plain world so thoroughly that he could not readily take in anything which did not seem in accordance with them. He expressed it thus:

Fact shall be fact for me, and the Truth the Truth as ever,
Flexible, changeable, vague, and multiform, and doubtful.—
Off, and depart to the void, thou subtle, fanatical tempter!

Clough's fate in life had been such as to exaggerate this naturally peculiar temper. His life and career were exactly those most likely to develop and foster a morbid peculiarity of intellect. He had an unusual difficulty in forming a doctrine as to the unseen world and he could not get the visible world out of his head. Too easily, one great teacher, Arnold, inculcated a remarkable creed; then another great teacher, Newman, took it away and then made him believe some of his own artificial faith; then it would not do. Clough thus fell back on that vague, impalpable, unembodied religion which I have attempted to describe. There was an odd cast to his mind. You never could tell whether it was that he would not show himself to the best advantage, or whether he could not. Few poets had a greater sense of the difficulty of finding truth. The stronger the passion for truth, the greater is the danger of ignoring the confusions of all things human:

> Rules baffle instincts—instinct rules,
> Wise men are bad—and good are fools,
> Facts evil—wishes vain appear,
> We cannot go, why are we here?

> O may we for assurance' sake,
> Some arbitrary judgement take,
> And wilfully pronounce it clear,
> For this or that 'tis we are here?

> Or is it right, and will it do,
> To pace the sad confusion through,
> And say:—It doth not yet appear,
> What we shall be, what we are here?

> Ah yet, when all is thought and said,
> The heart still overrules the head;
> Still what we hope we must believe,
> And what is given us receive;

Must still believe, for still we hope
That in a world of larger scope,
What here is faithfully begun
Will be completed, not undone.

My child, we still must think, when we
That ampler life together see,
Some true result will yet appear
Of what we are, together, here.

As a disciple of Wordsworth, Clough had a further difficulty in an age of ornate poetry, arising from an over-cultivated taste. To those who knew him, he had a very special charm. His conversation, like his poetry, had what might be called a pleasant cynicism, if cynicism did not have such a bad name. The ill nature and other offensive qualities which have given it that name were utterly out of Clough's way. If his opinions were often cynical his feelings were not. He was deficient not in moral feeling but in moral certainty. Without much fame, he had no envy. But he had a strong realism. He saw what it is considered cynical to see—the absurdities of many persons, the pomposities of many creeds, the splendid zeal with which missionaries rush on to teach what they do not know, the wonderful earnestness with which most incomplete solutions of the universe are thrust upon us as complete and satisfying. 'L'ironie', says the French novelist, 'est le fond du caractère de la Providence.' Clough knew what that meant and the truth it contained.

Undeniably this is an odd world, whether it should have been so or no; and all our speculations upon it should begin with some admission of its strangeness and singularity. The habit of dwelling on such thoughts as these will not of itself make a man happy, and may make unhappy one who is inclined to be so. In his time, Clough felt more than most men the weight of the unintelligible world. But such thoughts make an instructive man. Several survivors, myself included, owe much to Clough's quiet question, 'Ah, then, you think—?' Many pretending creeds, and many wonderful demonstrations, passed away before that calm inquiry. He had a habit of putting your own doctrine concisely before you, so that you might see what it came to, and that you did not like it. Even now that he is gone, some may feel the recollection of his society a check on unreal theories and half-mastered thoughts. I think of him now in his own words in the hope that they be true:

> Some future day when what is now is not,
> When all old faults and follies are forgot,
> And thoughts of difference passed like dreams away,
> We'll meet again, upon some future day.

⁂

Like Clough, I have no absorbing image of God, no pressing sense of His omnipotence, no vision of paradise or mankind perfected. Gazing after the infinite essence, we are like men watching through the drifting clouds for a glimpse of the true heavens on a drear November day. Layer after layer passes from our view, but still the same immovable grey rack remains. Still, unlike my lost friend, I have not retreated into a fatigued way of looking at great subjects. Though resigned to the dark realities which form the skeleton of our lives, I have sought to reconcile old religion and the new world, to bring together the spiritual and material, living humbly in the one, moderately in the other, and humanly in both. If my life has been shaped by an ideal, it has been the Aristotelian ideal of working towards contentment through the full and varied exertion of one's entire intellectual and moral nature, and forging a career in which the concept of a life should be practical without being worldly, many-sided without being superficial, religious without being visionary.

My own faith cannot be called exalted or mystical, and has little in the way of intensity; it does not presume to know too much of the spiritual; but it is respectful of the past, which is vital to a life of wise and moderate conduct. Modern civilisation is a world of pride and presumption; its fundamental problems are those which pass from generation to generation. If there be any truly painful fact about the world now tolerably well established by ample experience and ample records, it is that an intellectual and indolent happiness is wholly denied to the children of men. Conscience is the condemnation of ourselves; we expect a penalty. How to be free from this is the question. The problem of mankind is man, and every means must be taken to strengthen his moral character, through early education and the ethical inspiration of serious literature. It is the duty of every generation to state the ancient truth in the manner which that generation requires; to state the old answer to the old difficulty; to transmit, if not discover; convince, if not invent; to translate into the language of the living, the truths first discovered by the dead.

My generation came into life when the great discoveries in our knowledge of the material world were either recently made, or were on the eve of being made. The enormous advances which have been made in material civilization were half anticipated. There was a vague hope in science. The boundaries of the universe, it was thought, would move. Active, ardent minds were drawn with extreme hope to the study of new moving power; a smattering of science was immeasurably less common then than now, but science exercised a stronger dominion, and influenced a higher class of genius. It was new, and men were sanguine.

In the present day, younger men are perhaps repelled in the opposite extreme. We live among the marvels of science, but we know how little they change us. The essentials of life are what they were. We go by train, but we are not improved at our journey's end; we look after the railways and neglect the place on the map. We have a superfluity of manufactures—excellent things, no doubt, but they do not touch the soul. Somehow, they seem to make life more superficial. With a half-wayward dislike, some in the present generation have turned from physical science and material things. 'We have tried these, and they fail,' is the feeling. 'How is the heart of man the better for galvanic engines and hydraulic presses? Leave us to the old poetry and the old philosophy; there is at least a life and a mind.'

It is the day after the feast. We do not care for its delicacies; we are rather angry at its profusions; we are cross to hear it praised. Men who came into active life early in this century were the guests invited to the banquet; they did not know what was coming, but they heard it was something gorgeous and great; they expected it with hope and longing. As Hazlitt said, 'they confounded a knowledge of useful things with useful knowledge'. An idea, half unconscious, pervades them, that a knowledge of the detail of material knowledge is extremely important to the mass of men; that all will be well when we have a cosmical ploughboy and a mob that knows hydrostatics. We shall never have it; but even if we could, we should not be much the better. The heart and passions of men are moved by things nearer to attainment. The essential nature is stirred by the essential life; by the real actual existence of love, and hope, and character, and by the real literature which takes in its spirit, and which is in some way its essence.

⁂

The essential nature of man is not two things, but one thing. We have not one set of affections, hopes, sensibilities to be influenced by the visible world, and a different one to be influenced by the invisible world. We are moved by grandeur, or we are not; we are stirred by sublimity, or we are not; we hunger after righteousness or we do not; we hate vice or we do not; we are passionate or not passionate; loving or not loving; our heart is dull, or it is wakeful; our soul is alive or it is dead. Deep under the surface of the intellect lies the stratum of the passions of the intense, simple impulses, which constitute the heart of man; there is the eager essence, the primitive desiring being. What stirs this latent being we know. In general it is stirred by everything. Sluggish natures are stirred little, wild natures are stirred much, but all are stirred somewhat. It is not important whether the object be in the visible or invisible world; whosoever hates what he has seen will hate what he has not seen. Creation is, as it were, but the garment of the Creator; whosoever is blind to the beauty on its surface will be insensible to the beauty beneath; whosoever is dead to the sublimity before his senses will be dull to that which he imagines; whosoever is untouched by the visible man will be unmoved by the invisible God.

The conspicuous evidence of history confirms that these are not new ideas. Everywhere, religious organisation has been deeply sensitive to this world. If we compare what are called sacred and profane literatures, the depth of human affection is deeper in the sacred. A warmth as of life is on the Hebrew, a chill as of marble is on the Greek. In Jewish history the most tenderly religious character is the most sensitive to life. Along every lyric of the Psalmist thrills a deep spirit of human enjoyment; he was alive as a child to the simple aspects of the world; the very errors of his mingled career are but those to which the open, enjoying character is most prone; its principle, so to speak, was a tremulous passion for that which he had seen, as well as that which he had not seen. 'For all things are yours, whether ... the world, or life, or death, or things present, or things to come.'

Every one who has religious ideas must have been puzzled by what we may call the irrelevancy of creation to his religion. We find ourselves lodged in a vast theatre, in which a ceaseless action, a perpetual shifting of scenes, an unresting life, is going forward; and that life seems physical, unmoral, having no relation to what our souls tell us to be great and good, to what religion says is the design of all things. Especially when we see any new objects, or scenes, or countries, we feel this. Look at the great tropical plant, with large leaves stretching everywhere, with a big beetle on a leaf, and a humming-bird on a branch and an ugly lizard just below. What has such an object to do with *us*—with anything we can conceive, or hope, or imagine? What *could* it be created for, if creation has a moral end and object? Or go into a gravel-pit, or stone-quarry. You see there a vast accumulation of dull matter, yellow or grey, and you ask, involuntarily and of necessity, what is all this waste and irrelevant production of material? Can anything seem more stupid than a big stone *as* a big stone, than gravel for gravel's sake? What is the use of such cumbrous, inexpressive objects in a world where there are minds to be filled, and imaginations to be aroused, and souls to be saved?

Some of the world seems designed to show a little of God; but much more seems also designed to hide Him and keep Him off. The reply is, that if morality is to be disinterested some such irrelevant universe is essential. An unmoral universe, a sun that shines and a rain that falls equally on the evil and on the good are essential to morality in a being free like man, and created as man was. A miscellaneous world is a suitable theatre for a single-minded life, and, so far as can be seen, the only one. Much religion is untrue. A superstitious mind permits a certain aspect of God's character to tyrannise over it, to absorb it. The soul becomes bound down by the weight of its own revelation. Such minds are incapable of true virtue. We should guard against forming too clear an image of God, for in so doing we are forced into a spiritual attitude that is strained and unnatural. We do not wish to believe that man's best light is darkness, but it is man's ignorance that makes man a sound moralist. It shows us that a latent Providence, a confused life, an odd material world, an existence broken short, are not real difficulties but real helps. They, or something like them, are essential conditions of a moral life to a subordinate being.

Why is God so far from us? This agonizing question has depressed many intellects since intellects began to puzzle themselves. Perhaps as a bold man once said, religion and morality are inconsistent. The moral part of God's character cannot be shown to us with sensible conspicuous evidence; it could not be shown to us as Fleet Street is shown to us without impairing the first prerequisite of disinterestedness, and the primary condition of man's virtue. And if the moral aspect of God's character must of necessity be somewhat hidden from us, other aspects of it must be equally hidden. An infinite being may be viewed under innumerable aspects. God has many qualities in His essence which the word 'moral' does not exhaust. The attractive aspects of God's character must not be made more apparent to such a being as man than His chastening and severer aspects. We must not be invited to approach the holy of holies without being made aware, painfully aware, what holiness is. We must know our own unworthiness ere we are fit to approach or imagine an infinite perfection. The most nauseous of false religions is that which affects a fulsome fondness for a Being not to be thought of without awe, or spoken of without reluctance.

The Creator is not fastidious in His distribution of vice and virtue. To an outside observer, most men seem to walk through life in a torpid sort of sleep. They are decent in their morals, respectable in their manners, stupid in their conversation. In the present world, the fundamental difficulties of life and morals are little discussed. Few think of them clearly, and still fewer speak of them much. But they cloud the brain and confuse the hopes of many who have never stated them explicitly to themselves and never heard them stated explicitly by others. Meanwhile, superficial difficulties are in everyone's mouth; we are deafened with controversies on remote matters which do not concern us; we are confused with 'Aids to Faith' which neither harm nor help us. A tumult of irrelevant theology is in the air which oppresses men's heads and darkens their future.

For such a calamity there is no thorough cure; it belongs to the confused epoch in an age of transition and is inseparable from it. But the best palliative is a steady attention to primary difficulties—if possible a clear mastery of them; if not, a distinct knowledge of how we stand respecting them. The shrewdest man in the world who ever lived tells us: 'If a man will begin with certainties, he shall end in doubts; but if he will be content to begin with doubts, he shall end in certainties.' The maxim is even more applicable to matters which are not of this world than to those which are:

Say not the struggle nought availeth,
   The labour and the wounds are vain,
The enemy faints not, nor faileth,
   As things have been, things remain.

If hopes were dupes, fears may be liars;
   It may be, in yon smoke concealed,
Your comrades chase e'en now the fliers,
   And, but for you, possess the field.

For while the tired waves, vainly breaking,
   Seem here no painful inch to gain,
Far back through creeks and inlets making,
   Comes silent, flooding in, the main,

And not by eastern windows only,
   When daylight comes, comes in the light,
In front the sun climbs slow, how slowly,
   But westward, look, the land is bright.

CHAPTER IX

The American Crisis and the English Constitution

THE crisis of American democracy was the world's leading drama when I became editor of *The Economist*. A host of issues—political and constitutional, social and commercial—were of interest to readers of the paper and to the wider public. Ever since the American Revolution, the English have had divided views on their transatlantic cousins, watching and waiting to see the results of the republican experiment. A steady stream of writers invoked the United States as either a model or a warning; radicals praised America in their campaign for reform; conservatives, fearful of the effects of propaganda from across the Atlantic, argued the case against. In most Englishmen, slavery touched a nerve; it was a blot upon civilization, a bar to progress and a source of deplorable demoralization to slaves and slave owners alike. My father was a passionate opponent of American slavery; so too was Mr Wilson, who railed against it as a 'curse and crime'; so too was Hutton, who was an enthusiast for the North out of a loathing for slavery.

My own views, routinely expressed in *The Economist*, were decidedly anti-slavery, though I was less than sanguine about the easy eradication of such an entrenched institution. Just before the outbreak of hostilities, I wrote that the true issue between the North and South was not about prohibiting and preventing the extension of slavery. If it were, it might be worth an obstinate struggle and even a long civil war if there were any reasonable prospect of ultimate success. But what ground was there for assuming that any such distinct and noble aim was in the heart of Lincoln's government when its members spoke of coercion? Lincoln contended for the right of Congress to make laws for all unannexed, unsettled and unadmitted territories—he had not taken up the high ground of saying that slavery should not be introduced into any new districts. The real issue between the North and South was not the abolition of slavery but the decision on whether a free-labour or a slave-holding republic should henceforth hold the reins and direct the policy of the great American Federation, or a chief part of it.

I had little sympathy for the South and its deeply ulcerated semblance of civilization, but believed that the solution to the American crisis was to be found in a negotiated independence of the slave states, not their subjugation through what became one of the most costly wars in history. Southern independence, in my view, offered a fairer prospect for the speedy extinction of slavery in North America than Southern subjugation, on the grounds that should the South become a separate state, with fixed boundaries, the further extension of slavery would be impossible. The area of the institution being thus circumscribed, its immediate decline and ultimate extinction might be looked for as the natural result; whereas with the success of the North, followed by the restoration of the Union, the South would once more have at its command the power of the Federal Government, with which it would continue to push forward its aggressions against former slaves.

At the end of the secession war, with its untold miseries, I fully expected the South to remain chaotic and in need of a social revolution to address its besetting problems. The circumstances were fraught with difficulties. The South lay at the feet of its Northern conquerors, who had to decide the fate of the secessionists. The victors had to deal with a dissolved Southern society, with a defective Constitution calculated to frustrate the exercise of central power. The former slaves remained at the mercy of perhaps the most degraded, ignorant, brutal, drunken and violent class that ever swarmed in a civilised country. My fear was that Southerners, bent on keeping freed slaves in bondage, would be successful in evading the full consequences of their admission that slavery was over by adopting indirect measures that were insidious, oppressive and unwise. Such monumental issues created a political crisis and the greatest moral challenge to the United States: how to change former foes into friends.

Although critical of President Lincoln during the war, I came to admire him by the end of it. Just when his character and genius gave both North and South hopes of reconciliation, a Southern murderer gave occasion for a further outbreak of sectional hatred and diminished the prospects of reconstruction. Lincoln was that unique executive, who was so shrewd that he steered his way amidst the legal difficulties piled deliberately in his path, and so good that he desired power only for the national ends. It took a President of genius to overcome the imperfections of the very Constitution to which he swore an oath. Lincoln combined such a degree of sagacity and sympathy that he attained a vast moral authority that made the hundred wheels of the Constitution move in one direction without exerting physical force. We do not know in history another such example of the growth of a ruler in wisdom as he exhibited. A good but benevolent temporary despotism, wielded by a wise man, was the very instrument the wisest would have desired for the United States.

Lincoln's assassination was one of the most significant events since Waterloo. It was not merely that a great man had passed away, but he had disappeared at the very time when his special greatness seemed almost essential to the world, when his death would work the widest conceivable evil, when the chance of replacing him approached nearest to zero. He had been removed in the very way almost alone among causes of death that could have doubled the political injury. At the end of the war, it was essential that the central government in Washington be strong, for if it was weak, things were likely to become violent. Unlike other Englishmen, who thought Lincoln's assassination might be used to advance the liberal cause, I was pessimistic about the future of the United States without exceptional leadership and a reformed Constitution.

I would have been content to see the collapse of the Union and the emergence of an independent South, as long as it did not resuscitate slavery. No one can doubt that this would have been of benefit to the North. The same energy and enterprise which made the North great in spite of the difficulties of a slave connection would carry it on still faster and further without the hampering incubus of continued union with the South. If the New England states were a separate community they would have an education, a political capacity, and an intelligence that the numerical majority of no equally numerous people has ever possessed. In a state of this sort, where all the community is fit to choose a sufficient legislature, it is almost easy to create that legislature. As an independent state with a cabinet government, the New England states would be as renowned in the world for political sagacity as they now are for diffused happiness.

But separation was improbable at the moment of greatest opportunity. It would have required a constitutional revolution, and Americans had persuaded themselves that their eighteenth-century Constitution was a work of providential genius with the moral weight of a religious document; yet it was a Constitution designed by fallible men who had glossed over the issue of slavery and who had devised no easy process by which secession was possible short of conflict. A more flexible Constitution might have prevented the Civil War; in the end it failed to avert it and exasperated the mischief. Nor could it prevent the continuation of many of the grievances that precipitated the war. The outdated document was woefully inapplicable to a post-war Union divided into bitterly opposed castes. The Constitution left the American public desiring union but not unity, which is not conducive to stable or efficient government. It served the Union—but at what cost?

Years after the formal end of slavery, reports of the unhappy status of the former slaves remain dispiriting. They are liberated from their old masters but unable to find new ones for themselves. Despised by the great mass of Northerners and actually detested by the Irish—hated at once with mortification of defeat and the bitterness born of destitution by those to whom they were not long ago both slaves and wealth—and exposed on all sides to ill-treatment and neglect, these unhappy victims of philanthropy and war are dying by thousands; numbers are shot on the slightest provocation or from sheer brutality by miscellaneous ruffians; numbers more sink under disease and famine; numbers emigrate northward, to fare no better. The law does not protect them; the civil authorities will not; the military authorities cannot.

But I do not wish to appear too severe. For all America's inability to resolve the calamity of reconstruction and the disabling effects of its Constitution, the Northern victory and the end of slavery showed the American character to good effect, a people rising from time to time above their system of government. Whilst I saluted the vanquished gallantry of the South, I felt a personal sympathy with the Northerners, who won, as Englishmen would have won, by obstinacy. Since the end of hostilities, there have been liberal constitutional amendments, including the Fifteenth, which entrusted the vote to former slaves. The Constitution of the United States would long ago have brought the nation to a bad end if Americans had not a moderation of action singularly curious in a land where superficial speech is so violent; if they had not a regard for law such as no great people have yet evinced, and surpassing ours. The United States is not a country in which, as the saying goes, 'the worst comes to the worst'. But if this great people could make so much of what has so many serious faults in it as the American Constitution, what might they not make of a Constitution in which all those faults had been remedied?

※◎※

The American crisis was essentially a crisis of the Constitution; it raised the thorny issue of comparative government, a subject that has agitated political thinkers on both sides of the Atlantic for a century. My own criticism of the American Constitution was the natural result of my interest in the collapse of the Union, which I believed the federal system of government aggravated. There is much in the Constitution of the United States that draws on British precedent, and much in the American character that is essentially Anglo-Saxon. But the ancient, unwritten and malleable English Constitution adapts to change seamlessly. The American Constitution, in contrast, is a rigid document unsuited to changing social conditions; it was born in a moment of confusion, framed by pressing necessity by two extreme plans for meeting that necessity. Like all written documents, it failed when applied to a state of things different from any which its authors ever imagined. No one in England is much impressed by arguments which tacitly assume that the limited clauses of an old state paper can provide for all coming cases, and for ever regulate the future.

A cardinal failing of the American Constitution is that it lacks the simplicity of a single sovereign authority, which the House of Commons provides in Britain. It provides safeguards against ill-considered legislation but it fosters inactivity, creates resentment, and risks delay. The division of powers makes Congress useless as a partner and dangerous as an opponent. The unwieldy system is founded on a mistaken interpretation of the English Constitution current in the eighteenth century, the theory of the separation of powers. It is so carefully poised that any disturbance in the political machinery stops it from working, and it lacks a defined authority to deal with unexpected events. The framers were anxious to resist the force of democracy—to control its fury and restrain its outbursts—and hoped to control it by paper checks and constitutional balances. But they created a system of ingenious devices, the most complicated imaginable, which simply aggravated the calamities of their descendants, as recent history illustrates.

No constitutional system with multiple sovereignties has resolved the difficulty of combining decisiveness and security. A federal union, in which each state is a subordinate republic and a source of disunion, is only likely to succeed in circumstances exceptionally auspicious. With their dual demands of unity and independence, the American system favours local suspicions at the expense of national efficiency. Clearly, a system of government that requires three-fourths of the disparate states to ratify a constitutional amendment is contentious. The framers had been so fearful of placing sovereign power anywhere that they devised a system by which the Constitution could only be changed by authorities outside it. That a minority of small states could stifle the will of the majority is a defect that induces paralysis. Obvious evils cannot be remedied and absurd fictions have to be invented to get around harmful clauses. The practical arguments and legal disquisitions in America are often like those of trustees carrying out a mis-drawn will—the sense of what they mean is good, but it can never be worked out fully or defended simply, so hampered is it by the old words of an odd testament.

If the British cabinet system excels in a concentrating effective power, the American presidential system is built for safety; it creates paper checks and balances and competing branches of government to ensure that the state does not degenerate into tyranny. But such a system simply slows down the process of government, making it more difficult to organize public opinion, and, most damagingly, erects barriers between the executive and the legislature. The separation of powers does not enliven legislators; isolated from the executive, they tend to antagonism. Their debates cannot depose a President and are thus prologues without a play. To belong to a debating club hanging on to the coat tails of the executive is unlikely to stir a noble ambition and encourages inactivity. Presidential government, by its nature, divides political life into an executive half and a legislative half, and by so dividing, makes neither half worth a man's having.

⚜

In thinking about the crisis of American government my mind turned naturally to comparisons with England. Mr George Lewes, who had just taken up his post as editor of the *Fortnightly Review*, asked me to his house in St John's Wood to discuss my ideas. The result was a series of articles published in the *Fortnightly*, which appeared together as *The English Constitution* in 1867. They were written against the background of the American constitutional crisis and the campaign for Parliamentary reform at home. Roughly speaking, they described the working of the English Constitution as it stood in the time of Lord Palmerston. Since that time there have been many changes, some of spirit and some of detail, which required a modest recasting of the book. A second edition, which appeared in 1872, contained a new introduction and brought readers up to date with political developments at home and abroad. Since 1872, there have been further developments, but my many occupations forbid me to recast the book again, so, with all its speculations and failings, it will have to serve.

The English Constitution offered a fresh look at the mysterious workings of the British government. The more I studied the American government with its competing sovereignties, the more I came to doubt the supposition that the excellence of the English Constitution turned on the principle of the separation of powers between King, Lords and Commons, or that the legislative, the executive and the judicial powers are quite divided. Moreover, the twaddle about the rise of democratic freedom— the mesmeric hymn of radicals and a staple of 'Yankee brag'— struck me as suitable for schoolchildren; it did not explain how our constitutional system functioned or how Englishmen had travelled towards a political democracy. I intended to clear away some of the undergrowth of irrelevant ideas that had gathered round the English Constitution.

Language is the tradition of nations; each generation describes what it sees, but it uses words transmitted from the past. When a great entity like the English Constitution has continued for centuries in connected outward sameness, but hidden inner change, every generation inherits a series of inapt words—maxims once true, but of which the truth is ceasing or has ceased. As a man's family go on muttering in his maturity incorrect phrases derived from a just observation of his early youth, so, in the full activity of an historical constitution, its subjects repeat phrases true in the time of their fathers, and inculcated by those fathers, but now true no longer. An ancient and ever-altering constitution is like an old man who still wears with attached fondness clothes in the fashion of his youth: what you see of him is the same; what you do not see is wholly altered. I wished to have a look at the old man undressed.

Constitutionally, I am a sceptic and have never assumed constitutions to be founts of eternal wisdom. The English Constitution, though a source of useful political habits, is a mass of fictions that usefully disguise inconsistent practices, an ingenious hypocrisy with an array of outmoded relics on the surface and an efficient modern machine below. It is not a cathedral of government constructed by English genius, but the work of a careless race which captures the imagination of the ignorant and satisfies the reason of the educated. We have made, or rather, stumbled on, a marvel of intelligible government, which superimposes the poetry of monarchy upon a burgeoning democracy. Complex in ritual and administration, it has been subtly effective over the centuries; essentially simple, it is rich in easy ideas that all can make out and few can forget.

When I began *The English Constitution*, most Englishmen believed that a tripartite separation of powers was the basis of any worthwhile constitutional system. Simple country people of my acquaintance held beliefs about the omnipotence of the Crown and the nobility which had been ingrained over the centuries. They no more thought of the origin of the monarchy than they did of the origin of the Mendip Hills. Such beliefs still had great influence, but were in sharp contrast to the realities that I witnessed in London. The book had its origins in my observations of the actual world of politics, my earlier studies of statesmen, and the strange workings of human instincts. Political business, after all, is transacted not by machines, but by living and breathing men, of various and generally strong characters, of various and strong passions. Unless you know something of these passions and these characters you are continually at fault. *The English Constitution* was not blinded by the conventional wisdom or the existing scholarship on the mechanics of the Parliamentary system, but was a meditation on the difficulties of governance by public discussion and the way in which those difficulties had been surmounted in England.

My own experience suggested that the theory of three branches—Kings, Lords and Commons—was a pompous conceit. Politics abhors nicety of division, and English institutions were better understood if divided into two classes: first, those which excite and preserve the reverence of the population—the *dignified* parts; and next, the *efficient* parts—those by which it works and rules. The former is very old and complex, the latter modern and decidedly simple. Both are indispensable. There are two great objects which every constitution must attain to be successful, which every old and celebrated one must have wonderfully achieved—every constitution must first gain authority, and then use authority; it must first win the loyalty and confidence of mankind, and then employ that homage in the work of government.

There are practical men who reject the dignified parts of government. They say they want only to attain results, to do business. A constitution is a collection of political means for political ends; and if you admit that any part of a constitution does no business, you admit that this part of the constitution, however dignified or awful it may be, is nevertheless in truth useless. And other reasoners, who distrust this bare philosophy, have propounded subtle arguments to prove that these dignified parts of old governments are cardinal components of the essential apparatus, great pivots of substantial utility; and so manufactured fallacies which the plainer school have well exposed. But both schools are in error. The dignified parts of government are those which bring it force—which attract its motive power. The efficient parts only employ that power. The comely parts of a government are those upon which its vital strength depends. They may not do anything definite that a simpler polity would not do better; but they are the preliminaries, the needful prerequisites of all work. They raise the army, though they do not win the battle.

※◈※

The most strange fact, though the most certain in nature, is the unequal development of the human race. If we look back to the early ages of mankind, such as we seem in the faint distance to see, we can scarcely conceive ourselves to be of the same race as those in the far distance. There used to be a notion—not so much widely asserted as deeply implanted—that perhaps in a decade or so, all human beings might without extraordinary appliances be brought to the same level. But now when we see by the painful history of mankind at what point we began, by what slow toil, what favourable circumstances, what accumulated achievements, civilized man has become at all worthy in any degree so to call himself—when we realize the tedium of history and the painfulness of results, our perceptions are sharpened as to the relative steps of our long and gradual progress.

We have in a great community like England crowds of people scarcely more civilized than the majority of two thousand years ago; we have others even more numerous such as the best people were a thousand years since. The lower orders, the middle orders, are still, when tried by what is the standard of the educated 'ten thousand', narrow-minded, unintelligent, incurious. It is useless to pile up abstract words. Those who doubt should go out into their kitchens: let an accomplished man try what seems to him most obvious, most certain, most palpable in intellectual matters, upon the housemaid and the footman, and he will find that what he says seems unintelligible, confused and erroneous— that his audience think him mad and wild when he is speaking what is in his own sphere of thought the dullest platitude of cautious soberness.

Great communities are like great mountains—they have in them the primary, secondary and tertiary strata of human progress; the characteristics of the lower regions resemble the life of old times rather than the present life of the higher regions. And a philosophy which does not ceaselessly remember, which does not continually obtrude the palpable differences of the various parts, will be a theory radically false, because it has omitted a capital reality—will be a theory essentially misleading, because it will lead men to expect what does not exist, and not to anticipate that which they will find.

Everyone knows these plain facts, but by no means everyone has traced their political importance. When a state is constituted thus, it is not true that the lower classes will be absorbed in the useful; they do not like anything so poor. No orator ever made an impression by appealing to men as to their plainest physical wants, except when he could allege or prove that those wants were caused by the tyranny of some other class. But thousands have made the greatest impression by appealing to some vague dream of glory, or empire, or nationality. The ruder sort of men will sacrifice all they hope for, all they have, for an idea—for some attraction which seems to transcend reality, which aspires to elevate men by an interest higher, deeper, wider than that of ordinary life.

It is very natural, therefore, that the most useful parts of the structure of government should by no means be those which excite the most reverence. The elements which excite the most easy reverence will be the theatrical elements, which appeal to the senses, which claim to be embodiments of the greatest human ideas. The only sort of thing which comes home to the mass of men is that which is brilliant to the eye; that which is seen vividly for a moment, and then is seen no more; that which is hidden and unhidden; that which is specious, and yet interesting—palpable in its seeming, and yet professing to be more than palpable in its results.

If the common folk of Somerset are any guide, it is the dull traditional habit of mankind that guides most men's actions and is the steady frame in which each new artist must set the picture that he paints. Other things being equal, yesterday's institutions are by far the best for today; they are the most ready, the most influential, the most easy to get obeyed, the most likely to retain the reverence to which they alone inherit, and which every other must win. The most imposing institutions of mankind are the oldest; and yet so changing is the world—so fluctuating in its needs—that we must not expect the oldest institutions to be now the most efficient. We must expect what is venerable to acquire influence because of its inherent dignity; but we must not expect it to use that influence so well as new creations apt for the modern world, instinct with its spirit, and fitting closely to life.

A change has taken place in our polity analogous to the change in the structure of society. A republic has insinuated itself beneath the folds of Monarchy. We live, as Tennyson says, in a 'crown'd Republic', whose 'crowning common-sense' has saved her many times. We have had in England an elective first magistrate for nearly as long as the Americans have had an elective first magistrate. The secret of the English Constitution may be described as the nearly complete fusion of the executive and legislative powers. Unlike America, it has the great merit of a single sovereign authority in the House of Commons with the cabinet as the connecting link. The dignified aspect of the House of Commons is altogether secondary to its efficient use. The Commons has legislative and teaching functions; it expresses the mind of the English people on all matters which come before it. Its principal function, however, is one which we know quite well, though our common constitutional speech does not recognize it: it is an electoral chamber, the assembly which chooses our President.

The executive Prime Minister is the head of the efficient part of the Constitution; the Queen is only the head of the dignified part. As I stated rather smartly in *The English Constitution*, a monarch without initiative or veto in our peculiar form of kingship has the right to be consulted, the right to encourage, and the right to warn. What the Queen herself would make of such ideas is a mystery; there is no reason to suppose that she takes an interest in the jottings of a Liberal journalist. But my views may disconcert her advisors who have to assess the import of the

Crown's vestigial powers. Gladstone mentioned the book to the Queen's Private Secretary, but what he thinks of it is to me unknown; I have never had Palace connections. Courtiers are a strange breed of secretive men, who believe that economists and 'calculators' wish to tear down the Palace curtains and expose the Queen as a mere mortal. They see enemies in profusion but seldom recognise their friends.

Despite being a 'calculator', I am alive to the monarchy as the fount of national stability, which can be justified on the grounds of convenience. The republican notion that the demise of royalty would usher in a commonwealth of emancipated citizens is a dreary flight of fancy given to Englishmen who have been infected by French and American abstraction. The Crown is of singular importance in a divided and contentious free state because it is the sole object of attachment which is elevated above every dispute and division. But to maintain that importance, it must create attachment. It did so fully as long as Prince Albert lived. His character and circumstances forbade him to attempt to attract momentary popularity; he possessed the quality of discretion, which is seldom appreciated till it is lost. When the function of the Court is well performed it is easy to forget, but when it is ill performed keeps itself much in our remembrance.

When I wrote *The English Constitution* the Prince of Wales was widely seen as an unemployed youth and the Queen had become invisible, which threatened to undermine the loyalty and confidence of her subjects. The Queen's disappearance into cloistered widowhood contributed to the outburst of anti-monarchical sentiment some years ago. It is of the essence that the showy parts of the Constitution be on display. The public ceases to believe in what it does not see. Without the Queen in England, the present English government would fail and pass away. When most people read that she walked on the slopes at Windsor—that the Prince of Wales went to the Derby—they imagine that too much prominence is given to little things. But they have been in error. Constitutional royalty acts as a *disguise*. It enables our real rulers to change without heedless people knowing it. A veiled republic is the most vivifying of all possible governments for a people accustomed to freedom but still uneducated. The masses of Englishmen are not yet fit for an elective government; if they knew how near they were to it, they would be surprised, and almost tremble.

The Treasury is the spring of business, but the monarch is the 'fountain of honour'. The use of the Queen, in a dignified capacity, is incalculable. She is the focus of moral and religious sentiment—a salutary social influence—and it is an accepted secret doctrine that the Crown does more than it seems to. The existence of this secret power is, according to abstract theory, a defect in our constitutional polity, but it is a defect incident to a civilization such as ours, where august and therefore unknown powers are needed, as well as known and serviceable powers. The Crown's apparent separation from business is that which removes it both from enmities and from desecration, which preserves its mystery, which enables it to combine the affection of conflicting parties—to be a visible symbol of unity to those still so imperfectly educated as to need a symbol. Mystery is its life. In a phrase in *The English Constitution*, which has come to be associated with my name, I wrote that 'we must not let daylight in upon magic'. Am I to be remembered, like a Frenchman, simply for *bons mots*?

Above all things our royalty is to be reverenced, and if you begin to poke about it you cannot reverence it. We must not bring the Queen into the combat of politics or she will cease to be reverenced by all combatants; she will become one combatant among many. When once the change in politics is made from the one heaven-appointed monarch to a divided, shifting, constitutional system, the romance of royalty tends to pass away. We are governed by a cabinet, but who ever found sentiment for a managing committee? A republic has only difficult ideas in government; a constitutional monarchy has an easy idea. It has a comprehensible element for the vacant many, as well as complex laws and notions for the inquiring few. To state the matter shortly, monarchy is a government in which the attention of the nation is concentrated on one person doing interesting actions. A republic is a government in which that attention is divided between many, who are all doing uninteresting actions. Accordingly, so long as the human heart is strong and the human reason weak, monarchies will be strong because they appeal to diffused feeling, and republics weak because they appeal to understanding.

A family on the throne is an interesting idea also. It brings down the pride of sovereignty to the level of petty life. The women—one half the human race at least—care fifty times more for a marriage than a ministry. All but a few cynics like to see a pretty novel touching for a moment the dry scenes of the grave world. A princely marriage is the brilliant edition of a universal fact, and as such, it rivets mankind. They say that the Americans were more pleased at the Queen's letter to Mrs Lincoln on the death of the President than at any act of the English government. It was a spontaneous act of intelligible feeling in the midst of confused and tiresome business. Just so a royal family sweetens politics by the seasonable addition of nice and pretty events. It introduces irrelevant facts into the business of government, but they are facts which speak to 'men's bosoms', and employ their thoughts.

A German reviewer of *The English Constitution* referred to England as 'Eine République in weissen glacé Handschuhe'. In our disguised republic, it is needful to keep the ancient show while we secretly interpolate the new political reality. The higher and more educated portion of the English people have come to comprehend the nature of constitutional government, but the mass still do not comprehend it and many still look to the sovereign as the government. I do not count as an anomaly the existence of our double government, with all its infinite accidents, though half the superficial peculiarities that are often complained of arise out of it. The coexistence of a Queen's seeming prerogative and a Downing Street's real government is just suited to such a country as this, in such an age as ours. So well is our real government concealed, that if you tell a cabman to drive to 'Downing Street' he likely will never have heard of it, and will not in the least know where to take you.

꧁꧂

The effect of our curious constitutional history upon our national character has been great; and its effect on the common idea of that character cannot be exaggerated. Half the world believes that the Englishman is born illogical, and that he has a sort of love of complexity in and for itself. They argue that no nation with any logic in it could ever make such a Constitution. And in fact no one did make it. It is a composite result of various efforts, very few of which had any reference to the look of the whole, and of which the infinite majority only had a very bounded reference to a proximate end. But though I deny that the English Constitution is the result of an illogical intellect, yet I concede that the spectacle of the beneficial puzzle of our Constitution is not a good teaching for symmetrical arrangements. Being in itself, as Englishmen think, so good and yet so illogical, it gives them a suspicion of logic.

Seeing that the best practical things Englishmen know are produced by an inexplicable process, they are apt to doubt the efficiency of any explicable process. And as far as the Constitution itself is concerned they are right in thinking it dangerous to apply it to quick and sweeping thoughts. You must take the trouble to understand the plan of an old house before you can make a scheme for mending it; simple diagrams are very well on an empty site, but not upstairs in a Gothic mansion. Any good alteration of our Constitution must be based on a precise description of the part affected. So far the English suspicion of conspicuous logic is true and well founded, but undeniably they have come to regard their Constitution not only as a precedent but as a model, and so have sometimes a confidence in analogous compromises, rather than in contrasted simple measures. But the half measure must be one we understand.

New complexity is detestable to the English mind; and let any one who denies it try to advocate some plan of suffrage reform at all out of the way, and see how long it will be before he counts his disciples upon the fingers of a single hand. Our history and its complex consequences made the great political question of the last decade exceedingly difficult, made it such that no perfect solution could be looked for, and that only a choice of difficulties was possible. The deference of the old electors to their betters was the only way in which our old system could be maintained. After the 1867 Reform Act, the grave question was: how far would this peculiar old system continue and how far would it be altered? I am afraid that I put aside at once the idea that it would be altered for the better. I did not expect that the new class of voters would be more able to form sound opinions on complex questions than the old voters.

CHAPTER X

Politics

A T the time of writing *The English Constitution*, I stood for
Parliament. My father did not attach great significance to
political ambition; my mother was more sanguine, for she wanted
me to enjoy a wider prominence than I had achieved through
journalism. For some years, I had an irrational conviction that I
should be Member of Parliament for Bridgwater, which diminished my interest in other constituencies, and no amount of
reasoning would get it out of my head. When several leading
politicians, who thought I might advance the Liberal cause,
encouraged me to contest Dudley in May 1865, I declined. But a
letter from Gladstone recommending my candidacy persuaded
me to stand for Manchester the following month, where my
acquaintance with business and support for free trade were
thought to stand me in good stead. I gave a speech at the Town
Hall to a large crowd in the city; it was badly received and I with-
drew. Despite Gladstone's recommendation, the electors could
not see me as their Member of Parliament. 'If he is so celebrated,'
they said, 'why does not Finsbury elect him?'

Notwithstanding Manchester's verdict, I stood for my
coveted Bridgwater in the summer of 1866—a borough now

disfranchised—which I thought I was destined to represent. In my home county, the prospects appeared more favourable, and I travelled to the constituency in June, where a crowd of several thousand people greeted me with enthusiasm. I can still call up the image of the nomination day, with all the excited people milling about with their hands outstretched. Was it my money or my person they wanted? On the morning of the election I was ahead, but by a rush to the polls in the afternoon I lost to the Conservative candidate by seven votes. Not long afterwards, there was another election. Hutton, who had groundless visions of me as a statesman, pressed me to contest the London University seat, which had been newly created by the 1867 Reform Act. I flirted with the proposition and wrote an address to the electors. In the end the University chose Mr Robert Lowe of my own side as her member. Rejection in the home of free trade, in my home county, and in my home university did not spur me to further efforts; I ceased to have any aspiration to enter Parliament.

My misguided political ambition was nonetheless instructive. It exhibited a maximum of conviction with the minimum of argument, exposing the absurdity of my vivid faith in my own prospects. I had allowed myself to be flattered and unduly influenced. A few of my friends puzzled over my decision to stand for Parliament, for they recognized it as inconsistent with my inner life and stated opinions. For a man of doubting temper, hesitant to adopt a creed, suspicious of haste and ardent for moderation, a career in today's politics, however agreeable to one's self-esteem, is fraught with difficulty. I am a moderate Liberal, rather between sizes in politics—too conservative for many Liberals and too liberal for many Tories. A want of faith in political action is unusual in Parliament today, and I am wanting in zeal. I am also deficient in the didactic and oratorical impulses which are necessary to candidates, who must lapse into insincerity to assuage the demos. I admit to a degree of cynicism about the voting public; acting is required in intercourse with the unlettered elector, but acting has never been my line.

My abortive political calling raised the issue of whether the advantages of a Parliamentary career outweighed the disadvantages for a man of my temperament. The great majority of people are of the opinion that a seat in Parliament is the best thing that any Englishman can achieve. On the other hand, an intellectual minority say that Parliament is mostly composed of dull, rich men, that it is fit for such, and only such, that an intellectual man would only waste his mind there, that he should keep to his own pursuits—to literature, or science, or philosophy. The traditional idea rests upon an abolished fact. It is thought that going into Parliament is a good way of making money. A century ago it was possible for a young man who started with very small means, but who had available brains, to arrive at considerable wealth. There were then many sinecure places of fair amount which could be combined till they came to a very good income indeed. But such a career is no longer possible. The sinecures upon which it was based have been abolished. If a man of ability wishes to make money he had better go anywhere else than into Parliament, for there is much more to be spent than made there.

The real gains of a seat in Parliament are not to be dismissed. First, a man gains in social standing. 'I wrote books,' said a politician of the last generation, 'and I was a nobody; I made speeches and I was nobody; I got into Parliament and I was somebody.' As long as English society considers a seat in Parliament a great social prize, a seat there will be looked for and coveted. And it is very natural that it should be so regarded—it is far more comprehensible to most people than eminence in science or literature. A common person, who reads little, has very little notion what the books of the day are about. He thinks but little of them, and does not much understand them when he does think. But no one can help thinking of Parliament; no one can help knowing, more or less, what is done there, and who are the famous men there. To take part in the government of the country—to be a member of the assembly which rules the country—is a distinction much more intelligible to most people than to have written a book or made a discovery in optics.

A Member of Parliament has another advantage, for he has the means of acquiring much valuable information which it is difficult to learn in other ways. There is a vast mass of political knowledge which is at all times most important, and which no reading, no newspapers, can supply. Personality, for instance, is a most important element in politics, and our newspapers are distinguished by an absence of personality; they do not lift the veil of private life; they do not tell the inner weakness of public men or the details of their 'habit as they live'. The knowledge of public men, so freely given by newspapers, is a knowledge of masks rather than realities—of actors as they seem on the stage, rather than those actors as they really are. But, of course, an incessant press dealing with real personalities would sicken its readers and would drive sensitive men from public life.

The further advantage of becoming a Member of Parliament is the acquisition of power, though not enough to satisfy men of eager minds and despotic temperament. They can take part in the business of legislation, and if they are knowledgeable and industrious, they can easily find work which will be in itself valuable, and which those around them will respect them for doing. If they aspire to and obtain office, they have of course much more power, but it is rarely the sort of power which the tyrannical disposition most desires. An English statesman can only in very rare cases impose on others original plans of his own. His work is either to co-operate in committee with other men, or to embody in legal form the ideas of other men. Even in administration he has to cope with many obstacles, and must consult with and consider many other minds. Still this power, even so lessened and so defined, is the sufficient object of a wise ambition.

It is not my object to speak lightly of the legislative duties of Parliament. They are so well understood, and so obvious, that we are apt to think of them as its only duties. We should expect from Parliament every year, *not* indeed astonishing reforms, *not* statutes that will be an era in the history of our legislation, but an adequate supply of moderately useful measures. We should expect some business either of actual legislation, or of inquiries that may result in legislation from each session—but then we must remember that *this* business will have the qualities of *all* business. It will look dull and uninviting; it will administer no excitement; every part of it will be entirely untheatrical. 'Tedious usefulness' is said to be 'the acme of civilization'; it certainly is one of the most important functions of Parliament.

For all the dullness of the legislative process, tranquillity is not the lot of statesmen in emerging democracies. Glory they may have; the praise of men; the approbation of their own conscience; the happiness which springs from the full occupation of every faculty and every hour; the intense interest with which dealing with great affairs vivifies the whole of existence; the supreme felicity of all allotted to men—that of feeling that they have lived the life and may die the death of the truest benefactors of their race. All these rewards they may aspire to; but repose, a sense of enduring security, comfortable and confident relaxation in the feeling that one is safe in port, which enables a man to say to his soul, 'Soul! thou hast much peace laid up for many years: eat, drink, be merry, and sleep', these blessings are not for either sovereigns or statesmen, at least in Europe, in our age of discussion and the common man.

A very high price is paid for the advantages obtained by Members of Parliament. A great defect of the House of Commons is that it has no leisure. Men who wish to get something special out of Parliament will find that they are involved in a vortex of late hours, of long committees, of long listening to others, of long delays in speaking themselves. Nor is this the worst. An influential member has not only to pay much money to become such, and to give time and labour, he has to sacrifice his mind too—at least the characteristic part of it, that which is original and most his own. This is in the nature of things. If you want to represent a constituency you must not go down to them and say, 'See, I have all these new ideas, of which you have no notion: these new plans, which you must learn and study.' If you hint at anything like this you will be rejected at once. On the contrary, you must say what they think only perhaps a little better than they could say it; advocate the schemes they wish advocated; be zealous for the Party's tradition. The cleverer you can be in doing this, the more likely you can please them with their own thoughts and make them happy with their own inventions, and the better they will like you. Exceptions apart, you must not try to teach them. They want a representative, not a tutor; a man who will vote as they wish, not one who will teach them what they ought to wish for.

The representative principle—the notion that candidates should spout the opinion of the common man rather than educated opinion—is the cause of the deluge of commonplaces that fill the newspapers at election time. In the million speeches which have been made by candidates in recent elections, it may be doubted if there have been a dozen original thoughts; even the best, as a rule, have only been old tunes admirably played. There is plenty of originality in England if it would pay to be original. But at an election it does not; you will only puzzle your constituency by saying what they do not understand, and offend them by seeming to think that you are wiser than they are. 'We never heard of such a thing in all our lives before,' they will say, and will think it a sufficient objection to the truth of an idea or the sufficiency of a plan. A man who wants to represent others must be content to seem to be as they are, and it will be better for him if he is as they are. If he wishes to enter Parliament he must be content to bind himself to the formularies of common thoughts and common creeds, or he will not succeed in his candidature. And to some minds there is no necessity more vexing or more intolerable than acting a part composed by the benighted.

※◎◎◎※

The Reform Act of 1867 encouraged the thespians. It is well known that I opposed the Bill and advised the government to reject it. As for the Liberal enthusiasts, I felt inclined to say 'go home, sir, and take a dose of salts, and see if it won't clear it all out of you'. It is one thing to admit the common man to a political dinner; it is another to admit him to the high-table feast. The contrast between Lancashire and Devonshire has never been greater. For decades the dangers of democracy have been centred in the industrial cities, where the majority live by wages, where they have no fixed property, where they have scarcely a fixed home, where they may be excited by agitators. Now such men threaten to swamp the instructed classes who mould the most enlightened public opinion. There is no infallibility in numbers, and one can foresee Britain becoming a worse America, in which the lower orders are equally despotic, but are not equally intelligent.

The Reform Act of 1867 will be remembered as long as the Constitution of England is remembered. Why so great a change was made so silently and with so little national discussion will amaze our children—just as we of this generation cannot comprehend the Reform discussions of 1832, and why so much was hoped from a measure upon its face so prosaic. The men who passed the Reform Act of 1867 had the characteristic virtues which enable Englishmen to effect great changes in politics: their courage and their disposition to give up something rather than to take the uttermost farthing. But in 1867 they displayed all the characteristic English defects: their want of intellectual and guiding principle, their even more complete want of the culture which would provide that principle, their absorption in the present difficulty, and their hand-to-mouth readiness to seek reform without thinking of the consequences. The moral is that these English qualities as a whole—merits and defects together—are better suited to an earlier age of politics than to today.

The Reform Act of 1867 shed a painful light on the Reform Act of 1832 and has exhibited in real life what philosophers said were its defects. While these defects lingered in the books they were matters of dull teaching, and no one cared for them. But now they are living among us. Disraeli is identified with the 1867 Reform Act. His name was the first on the back of the Bill of the names of those who brought it in, and will be the name which posterity will associate with it. And the reward is just. It is Disraeli's Bill. So much is certain. He wished all along to go down very low, to beat the Whigs—if possible, the radicals too—by basing the support of the Conservative Party upon a lower class than those which they could influence. To this end he induced his party to surrender their creed and their policy; he altered what his followers had to say, even more than the Constitution under which they are to live. How then did he attain such a singular success?

It is usual to say that he attained it by fraud and deceit, and I am not about to defend his morality. But a little study of human affairs is enough to show that fraud alone does not succeed; it is too ugly and coarse for man to bear; it is only when disguised in great qualities and helped on by fine talents that it prospers. Disraeli is one of the most observant students of human life in England. He has had to struggle; and this has no precedent; he is the one literary adventurer who has led the House of Commons. In the course of his aspiring youth he observed all classes of men in their plain traits. The whole of this observant faculty, which was trained in social life, has been concentrated on Parliament. As the leader of his party, he has charmed the House, and has given a literary flavour to the debates in which he took part. But it has been his misfortune throughout his political career to lead a party of very strong prejudices and principles, without feeling himself any cordial sympathy with either the one or the other. It remains a great mystery how such a man came to rule a party of squires.

Disraeli is not profound in the least, and perhaps he would laugh at telling what he thinks is his best creed. But he has a fatal facility in suggesting hazy theories which would puzzle an Aristotle. The driest and hardest thinker could never get right if he persisted in tying his words into the pretty puzzles which Disraeli delights in. His language on abstract rights is to that of a thinker by profession—say Mill—what discolouring artificial light is to daylight. You never know what he is talking about, or whether it means much or little. But, though not deep, Disraeli's mind is beyond measure quick, and, as far as it penetrates, original. There is nothing routine about him. He got the House of Commons to sit at unheard-of hours—from 2 till 7—and seemed to think nothing of it, though some grave members thought it almost a Reform Bill in itself. It has been said that the best general is he who best knows how to repair a defeat; and if that were translated, it might be said that Disraeli has been the best leader of the House of Commons, for he knows how to glide out of a scrape better than anyone.

If we look at Disraeli's legislative policy, we cannot avoid the criticism that while it was in one great instance at least not a policy favourable to his own party, it affected to be so, and was forced upon them on the plea that it would prove so. He proposed a policy which would 'dish the Whigs', but which was not really Conservative and which dished the Conservatives; and so he had neither the party success of a clever strategic move, nor the national success of sacrificing party to the people's welfare. With regard to the Reform Act this was conspicuously the case. What he proposed to do for party objects failed to achieve those objects. And, unfortunately, he never professed or proposed to sink party in the welfare of the nation. Disraeli has nothing of the statesman's power of imaging forth the actual effect and operation of the measures he advocates—nothing of the statesman's power of penetrating to the heart of a deep national conviction. He would sooner commit himself to the tender mercies of popular forces of which neither he nor any other man has really fathomed the scope. To the mass of common Englishmen, who do not regard Parliamentary proceedings as a game, Disraeli is simply unintelligible. He ruled the country by ruling Parliament, but he has never had any influence in Parliament reverberating from the nation itself.

≈≋◉≋≈

The sudden extension of the franchise is one of those facts of the first magnitude which are never long resisted. In my address to the electors for the University of London seat in 1868, I discussed some of the questions before the country at the time. It was necessary to swallow my objections to the Reform Act—the seat I was contesting resulted from it—but it was not a terrible trial to strike a political bearing amenable to my audience of educated voters. After the 1832 Reform Act, I submitted, the cry was, 'Register! Register! Register!' After 1867, it was 'Educate! Educate! Educate!' If the labours of the Parliament of 1832 were labours of demolition, the work of the new Parliament would be the work of reconstruction. But there remained 'organic' questions which were not set to rest by the 1867 Reform Act. We still not only had to discuss how we should use our government, but also what should be the scope and structure of our government.

After 1867, the work was more difficult, more delicate, more gradual, than that of our fathers; they had mostly to pull down what they knew to be evil; we had tentatively and slowly to erect what we hoped would be good.

The natural impulse of the English people is to oppose authority—our freedom is the result of centuries of resistance to executive power—but after the 1867 Reform Act the English state is now but another name for the English people. The secure predominance of popular power mitigated our traditional jealousy of executive government. From countless causes the great cities in the North of England, which still have far too little weight as compared with the stationary South, will demand a stronger central government. In a society in which the inhabitants of those cities are now for the first time directly represented, the state is now intervening far more widely than previously in lessening vice and misery. The material necessities of this age require a strong executive; a nation destitute of it cannot be as healthy or vigorous as a nation possessing it. As a consequence, we are undergoing an expansion in the size of government. Inevitably, the ensuing bureaucracy will care more for routine than for results. A bureaucracy is sure to think that its duty is to augment official power, rather than to leave free the energies of mankind; it overdoes the quantity of government, as well as impairing its quality.

The English rarely honour the mind, and over the decades political reformers have destroyed intellectual constituencies without creating new ones. Thus by conspicuous action they taught mankind that an increase in the power of numbers was the change most to be desired in England. And of course the mass of mankind are only too ready to think so. The poor in our industrial cities are inclined to believe their own knowledge to be 'for all practical purposes' sufficient, and to wish to be emancipated from the authority of a higher culture. The growing severance of

Englishmen from life in contact with the natural world, which in previous ages had shaped the mind and stabilized the social fabric of our island race, must have consequences. What we now have to do, therefore, is to induce this self-satisfied, stupid, inert mass of men to admit its own insufficiency, which is very hard; to recognize fine schemes for redressing that insufficiency, which is harder; and to exert ourselves to get those ideas adopted, which is hardest of all. Such is the duty which reformers have cast upon us.

The higher culture has little say in England, for only the loudest sort of expression is permitted to attain its due effect. The popular organs of the press so fill men's minds with incomplete thoughts that deliberate treatment, that careful inquiry, that quiet thought, have no hearing. People are so deafened with the loud reiteration of many half-truths that they have neither curiosity nor energy for elaborate investigation. The very word 'elaborate' has become a reproach. Elaboration produces something which the mass of men do not like, because it is above them—which is tiresome, because it needs industry; difficult, because it wants attention; complicated, because it is true. English thought has rarely been so unfinished, so piecemeal, so *ragged* as it is now. We have so many little discussions that we get no full discussion; we eat so many sandwiches that we spoil our dinner.

The unthinking mass of common people, without distinction of party, had no conception of the effect of the Reform Act of 1867. It did not stop at skilled labour. And no one will contend that the ordinary working-man who has no special skill, and who is only rated because he has a house, can judge much of intellectual matters. We have not enfranchised a class less needing to be guided by their betters than the old class; on the contrary, the new class needs it more than the old. The real question is: will they submit to it, will they defer in the same way to wealth and rank, and to the higher qualities of which these are the rough symbols and common accompaniments? In answering this question, statesmen have now a great responsibility. If they raise questions which will excite the lower orders of mankind; if they raise questions on which those orders are likely to be wrong; if they raise questions on which the interest of those orders is not identical with the interest of the state, they will have done the greatest harm they can do.

The future of this country depends on the happy working of a delicate experiment. If the first duty of the poor voters is to try to create a 'poor man's paradise', as poor men are apt to fancy that paradise, the great political trial now beginning will simply fail and the wide gift of the elective franchise will be a great calamity to the whole nation. In the meantime, our statesmen have the greatest opportunities they have had for many years, and likewise the greatest duty. They have to guide the new voters in the exercise of the franchise, to guide them quietly, and without saying what they are doing, but still to guide them. The leading statesmen in a free country have great momentary power. They settle the conversation of mankind. In conjunction with their counsellors, they settle the programme of their party. It is by that programme that the world forms its judgment. The common ordinary mind is quite unfit to fix for itself what political question it shall attend to; it is as much as it can do to judge decently of the questions which drift down to it; it almost never settles its topics; it can only decide upon the questions of those topics.

It is for our principal statesmen to lead the public, and not to let the public lead them. No doubt when statesmen live by public favour, as ours do, this is a hard saying, and it requires to be carefully limited. I do not mean that our statesmen should assume a pedantic and doctrinaire tone with the English people; if there is anything which the English people thoroughly detest, it is that tone exactly. And they are right in detesting it; if a man cannot give guidance and communicate instruction formally without telling his audience 'I am better than you', then he is not fit for a guide.

But much argument is not required to guide the public, still less a formal exposition of that argument. What is mostly needed is the manly utterance of clear conclusions; if a statesman gives these in a felicitous way he has done his part. He will have given the text, the scribes in the newspapers will write the sermon. A statesman ought to show his own nature, and express what is to him important truth. And so he will both guide and benefit the nation. But if, in a time when great ignorance has an unusual power in public affairs, he chooses to accept and reiterate the decisions of that ignorance, he is only the hireling of the nation, and does little save hurt it.

It will be said that this is obvious, and that everybody knows that 2 and 2 make 4, and that there is no use in inculcating it. But I answer that the lesson is not observed in fact. My great fear after the 1867 Reform Act was that both our political parties would bid for the support of the working-man; that both of them would promise to do as he liked if he would only tell them what it was; that, as he now holds the casting vote in our affairs, both parties would beg and pray him to give that vote to them. I could conceive of nothing more corrupting or worse for a set of poor ignorant people than that two combinations of well-taught and rich men should constantly offer to defer to their decision, and compete for the office of executing it. *Vox populi* will be *Vox diaboli* if it is worked in that manner.

My imagination conjures up a contrary danger. I can conceive that questions might be raised, which, if continually agitated, would combine the working-men as a class together. In all cases it must be remembered that a political combination of the lower classes for their own objects is an evil of the first magnitude; that a permanent combination of them would make them (now that so many of them have the suffrage) supreme in the country; and that their supremacy, in the state they now are, means the supremacy of ignorance over instruction and of numbers over knowledge. So long as they are not taught to act together, there is a chance of this being averted, and it can only be averted by the greatest wisdom and the greatest foresight of the higher classes. They must not only avoid every evil, but every appearance of evil; while they have still power they must remove, not only every actual grievance, but, where it is possible, every seeming grievance too; they must willingly concede every claim which they safely concede, in order that they may not have to concede unwillingly some claim which would impair the safety of the country.

∞⊕≈

The nation has reached a time when one of the most important qualifications of a Prime Minister is to exert direct control over the masses. It was fortunate that the election of 1868 restored Gladstone to power. My earlier criticisms of him had moderated, and I believed that if the Reform Act had any merit it would augment the Liberal Party. Gladstone's wonderful gifts had long charmed the nation. In amplitude of knowledge, in intensity of labour, in a flexible eloquence suited either to the highest discussions or to the meanest details of public business, he has no living equal; and it is no light matter that he has led the House of Commons with an eager and noble morality which has awakened all the nation. In today's politics, how quickly a leading statesman can change the tone of the community. As it happened, Gladstone's skills as a great popular orator added greatly to the strength of the government's position.

But the government of Gladstone confirmed that tranquillity is not the lot of those who rule in modern days. The Reform Act settled only one dispute and in so doing raised a series of new ones. The change in recent years is less a change of particular details than of pervading spirit. A new world has arisen which is not as the old world, and we naturally ascribe the change to the Reform Act. But this is easily overstated. If there had been no

Reform Act at all there would, nevertheless, have been a change in English politics. There has been a change of the sort which, above all, generates other changes—a change of generation. The Reform Act cleared the room for the emergence of new issues. A political country is like an American forest: you have only to cut down the old trees, and immediately new trees come up to replace them; the seeds were waiting in the ground, and they began to grow as soon as the withdrawal of the old ones brought in light and air. These new issues of themselves would have made a new atmosphere, new parties, new debates. We are now engulfed in educational reform, the question of the Church, the problem of Ireland, and women's rights.

To address these issues what is needed is not a new middle party, which in the country would seem an unintelligible nondescript, but a middle government, which would represent the common element between the two parties. Neither party should be able to govern in the spirit, or according to the wishes, of its extreme supporters. Thus far, my fears that the working classes would take all the decisions to themselves—would combine as a class and legislate for their class interests—have not been realised. In many respects the working of recent changes has not been beneficial. At no time, perhaps, was the influence of money so great; at none, was the difficulty so great of introducing *mind* into Parliament. But on the cardinal point, and that most feared of all, the effect of the new laws, as yet at least, is less than either friends or enemies expected. In the main, things go on much as before. The predominance remains as yet where it ought to be: in the hands of leisure, of property and of intelligence.

The rise of popular government promotes excitement, and nothing is so dangerous to a nation's stability as the habit of uniting thought and excitement, which, if history is a guide, leads to the fervent advocacy of unattainable ideals. To sustain a steady and successful culture like England, all political changes should be made slowly and after long discussion. Public opinion should be permitted to ripen upon such issues as further Parliamentary reform, church reform or land reform. And the reason is that all the important English institutions are the relics of a long past; they have undergone many transformations; like old houses which have been altered many times, they are full of both conveniences and inconveniences which at first sight would not be imagined. Very often a rash alterer would pull down the very part which makes them habitable, to cure a minor evil or improve a defective outline. Still, the English have a genius for the compensation of errors, which may need to be called upon in future, for many of the recent alterations to our politics have been hasty and ill conceived.

With characteristic wisdom Lord Melbourne's habitual question was 'can't you let it alone?' Statesmen in modern days take on board too much and modern people burden themselves with unnecessary responsibilities. Until men have sufficiently verified the principles on which action ought to proceed it is wise not to proceed on great enterprises, whether at home or abroad. At *The Economist* we have consistently opposed British engagement in European quarrels. We should remain well armed but detached, ready to mediate but not to intervene. Beyond our shores, trade, not power, is our national interest. I have no desire to pull down the Empire, but I am suspicious of an ambitious foreign policy and cannot justify the financial risk of foreign entanglements. As I have said privately, I would be content to find an excuse to give up India, to throw the Colonies on their own resources, and to see the English people accept the place of a lesser European power. This is not an unpatriotic wish but a course which would raise the national mind and make the English a more leisurely race.

CHAPTER XI

Physics and Politics

M Y friend Sir George Cornewall Lewis, who was an odd mixture of amusing anomalies, used to say, 'the world would not be a bad place if it were not for its pleasures'. I have never been one to enjoy invented delights, but prefer the cause- less happiness that comes from the intuitive impulses of a feverish brain. Still, even a playful mind has its cares and stresses. My life has not been quiet, rushing among the details of our time. Thus holidays have been an escape, though my forbearing wife, who has a taste for travel, has had to put up with my frequent disap- pearances to finish a pressing piece of work. There have been tours of French churches, climbing in the Dolomites, revisiting places in Devon and Cornwall which I thought most beautiful as a child—I have an especial fondness for the coast at Lynmouth. The love of rural landscapes has been among my most pleasur- able sensibilities, which the scenes drawn by Wordsworth and Scott—medication for my state of mind—have made all the more beautiful.

In the autumn of 1867, we spent several weeks in the Pyrenees, which has the charm of the golden light of the southern sun. The north-west corner of Spain is a better sort of Devonshire, the finest of our counties. Indeed, the country round San Sebastian is the only place I should like to live outside England. My nature by early use and long habit soon feels the want of a certain kind of scenery and is apt to be alarmed at perpetual snow and all sorts of similar beauties. But in the Pyrenees, the sun has some secret effect that makes one inclined to be pleased, and the light lies upon everything and one fancies that one is charmed only by the outward loveliness.

Our return from Spain to a cold and damp England was a shock to my system; at Christmas I caught a chill which developed into a severe attack of internal inflammation. Though my health had been delicate for some years, this was my first serious illness. Throughout the winter I was too weak to work. In March we removed to Lyme Regis but the relapses persisted. To reduce my labours at *The Economist*, I engaged the able statistician Robert Giffen. With my aversion to detail and weak eyesight, I deputed him to write the weekly article on the money market and the statistical reports, while I managed to keep abreast of the more general economic and political affairs. I was still ailing at the time of the 1868 election. Few of the electors of the University of London knew that my address to them was written in a state of precarious health.

I suffered another serious relapse in August 1869. Eliza, whose life has been given over to my comfort, looked after me with great solicitude; meanwhile, various friends, including Arnold, Hutton and Greg, made frequent visits to my bedside. As ever, the physicians prescribed unemployment, which I waved away with my customary obstinacy. The tiring journey to my office in the Strand was impossible, but I managed to carry on at *The Economist* by dictation and my colleagues visited me at home to ensure that things carried on much as normal at the paper. Poetry readings and a few recuperative drives on Wimbledon Common lifted my spirits, and after some weeks

I recovered sufficiently to join my wife at Ostend for a brief holiday. A planned tour of Germany had to be postponed, but by the autumn I was well enough to give evidence to the Bribery Commission at Bridgwater, at which it was said that I was the only person to come out of it unscathed. At the beginning of 1870, in order to get more riding, we moved from Upper Belgrave Street to the Poplars on Wimbledon Common, where my sister-in-law Emilie and her husband Russell Barrington resided.

⚜

On 21 February 1870 my mother died unexpectedly of influenza at Herd's Hill. I received the news from my brother-in-law on Cannon Street Station and rushed back to Somerset to be with my father, who was devastated by our loss. 'It looks a very desolate home without her,' he said mournfully. And so it was. Her death eclipsed everything at the time; I was irrevocably cut off from my youth, a hopeless companion, distracted in London, aimless in Langport. After all my mother had meant to me, it was difficult to think of life without her. Over the years our roles had become reversed. I had come to take a parental interest in her state of mind, while she had become dependent on my affection and judgment. I felt her death all the more painfully because she died without the happiness of having grandchildren. At the funeral many people looked upon her death as a relief. No one who loved her would have entertained such an idea.

> This world is the nurse of all we know,
>   This world is the mother of all we feel,
> And the coming of death is a fearful blow
>   To a brain unencompassed with nerves of steel;
> When all that we know or feel, or see,
> Shall pass like an unreal mystery.

The secret things of the grave are there,
   Where all but this frame must surely be,
Though the fine-wrought eye and the wondrous ear
   No longer will live to hear or to see
All that is great and all that is strange
In the boundless realm of unending change.

Who telleth a tale of unspeaking death?
   Who lifteth the veil of what is to come?
Who painteth the shadows that are beneath
   The wide-winding caves of the peopled tomb?
Or uniteth the hopes of what shall be
With the fears and the love for that which we see?

⁂

I have a tendency to retreat into my own mind, and my mother's death and my chronic illness would have been unbearable without the support of family and friends. It has been my good fortune to have a number of companions who care for my welfare and know my mind, who accept my contrariness and tolerate my jests. Where would I have been without Clough and Hutton to correct my opinions and dampen my spirits? I confess to having little compassion for the toiling masses of unknown men, whose lives are mired in misery and pain. Even when people wish to feel compassion, it is more often a desire than an actual emotion. Perhaps my lifelong anxieties about my mother's condition ate away at my sympathies. I sometimes feel that each of us is born with a measure of compassion, which is easily exhausted in this suffering world. 'Nous avons tous assez de force pour supporter les maux d'autrui.'

My friendships have often been bound up with politics. While Liberals are to my taste, I have long had an affinity with moderate, intellectual Tories, who have that cavalier capacity for enjoying life. The reproaches that I had levelled at the Conservatives of Lord Eldon's time were no longer apt, for the Tories were no longer the party of fear, and a spirit of earnestness has gone out into society, which has moderated the diffusion of recklessness and selfishness. Lord Carnarvon, who is one of my sort, and has run to mind, has been a friend for many years. As a leader of the Conservative peers who opposed Disraeli's Reform Bill he had kept me informed on that crisis. Lady Carnarvon, who died not long ago, was a woman of great charm, with snaps of literature, who could break through the conventional formalities into genuine conversation. Their parties at Highclere were my first experience of a 'great house', and the mix of intellectuals and fast people is always entertaining, if sometimes alarming. My avowed purpose at these gatherings has been to keep my character for 'wisdom' and 'respectability'.

My friendship with George Lewes has been enduring since his time as editor of the *Fortnightly* a decade ago. Over the years, I have made frequent visits to the Priory in St John's Wood, where I have taken much pleasure from his company and that of George Eliot, our greatest living writer of fiction, who seems unfitted for ordinary society and thus holds court on Sunday afternoons to a stream of visitors. She is a rare physiological study, too large and weighty for the conventional world and rather strange in respect to its small amenities. Our conversations ranged widely, from the money market to literary matters and sometimes took an intimate turn about her difficulties in composition. She would speak about the 'pain' it caused her, though to readers her logical style seems effortlessly to complement her sense of proportion.

⚶⚶

My ill health and failure to enter Parliament did not diminish my interest in politics. There is a natural fascination in what Macaulay called 'the grinding, the invidious, the closely-watched slavery, which is marked by the name of power'. In *The Economist*, I made utterances on the historic importance of statesmen, Irish Home Rule, and Jacob Bright's Bill to abolish the electoral disabilities of women. The question of female suffrage shared the benefit of that tendency in favour of change as change, which sprang up with the passage of the Reform Bill and has greatly increased since. It is no argument now against a measure or an amendment that it is new. The presumption rather is, even among many Conservatives, that there are defects in the old arrangements, and that new and old should be discussed on their merits, which gives an obvious advantage to what is new.

No doubt the notion of women having votes is a very considerable innovation; in my own family of cultivated females the idea meets with little enthusiasm. The enfranchisement of women is contrary to recognized usages and habits in a more than ordinary degree; as in all questions between the sexes, there is a difficulty in making them the subject of common reasoning at all. The argument that female influence would be retrograde—that the constituencies would be more Conservative—was not an objection of merit, though it weighed with some in the Liberal Party. There was a good deal to be said for Bright's Bill. The measure did not violate the general policy and dealt with a minority who fulfilled every obligation of citizenship exactly as men. Had it passed, it would have removed an anomaly in our electoral system and the balance of probabilities was that it would have done some good by bringing a wholly fresh element into political life.

The issue of votes for women raised another anomaly in our culture—the want of university degrees for women. If one is to believe elements in the press, the idea of opening degrees to women is to force women into duties for which they are totally unfitted. It is the wildest idea conceivable that because women are educated, and afford evidences of a good education, they will be more likely to lose their feminine qualities than they are in their present condition of relative ignorance. Is it ignorance which causes feminine grace, or, rather, which prevents it? No doubt an additional weapon is always an advantage in the battle of life, and women with knowledge will be able to take posts which they could not pretend to take without knowledge. Yet why should not such posts be rather more instead of less becoming to them as women, than those into which they are, as it were, *forced* by their deficiency in knowledge.

It is greatly to be desired that a higher education will qualify women for occupations from which they are at present prohibited. I believe that no women are so little likely to be forward and presumptuous as those who have received an education above their fellows. Instead of encouraging them to pass into conflicts for which they are not fitted, it will, I believe, tend to a very remarkable degree to put a drag on that excitable and dangerous feminine enthusiasm which is so marked a feature of our time, not because the leaders are educated, but because they are uneducated. I sincerely trust that the University of London will soon be granting degrees for women. The result would be a small but valuable addition to the powers and interests of women, and would act advantageously on the social life of the day. The frivolity of women is one of the greatest causes of vice and frivolity in men. If we can but have a generation of women somewhat less dull, and somewhat less inclined to devote themselves to silly occupations, we hope that not only their children but their husbands and brothers will be the gainers.

※⊚※

Physical restrictions shifted my focus to speculative subjects which had occupied me since my days at university. Indeed, the research of scientific authorities had intrigued me since my schooldays at Bristol College with Dr Prichard, who was among those ethnologists who had dug out of the dim past actual facts concerning the history of human races. Soon after the publication of *The English Constitution*, I began to work on *Physics and Politics*, which applied the latest scientific and historical discoveries to the realms of society and politics. It first appeared, like its predecessor, as instalments in the *Fortnightly*. My protracted weakness necessitated a shorter work than I had imagined and interrupted its publication as a book, which appeared, with the editorial support of John Morley, in 1872.

The book developed some of the issues raised in *The English Constitution*, which had been illuminated by the writings of Charles Darwin, Sir Henry Maine, Sir John Lubbock and Herbert Spencer, among others. My aim was to explain the evolution of societies, to illustrate the psychological foundations of collective action, and to suggest the significance of imitation, co-operation, discussion and natural selection between competing social groups. What were the political prerequisites of progress, and especially early progress? How had societies moved from the yoke of custom, which typified ancient communities, to the age of discussion, which exemplifies the modern world? Why, in particular, had European nations been able to free themselves from the elaborate framework of tradition, taboo and religious sanction that inhibited the progress of other civilizations?

Our habitual instructors, our ordinary conversation, our inevitable and ineradicable prejudices tend to make us think that 'Progress' is the normal fact in human society. But history refutes this. The ancients had no conception of progress; they did not so much as reject the idea; they did not even entertain the idea. Oriental nations attained a comparatively high level of civilisation before they became petrified by custom, but for centuries they have been what they are. Only a few nations of European origin have advanced; and yet these think—seem irresistibly compelled to think—such advance to be inevitable, natural and eternal. Why then this great contrast? What I attempted was a solution to this question through a discussion of the principles which tend towards progress.

I do not pretend that I fully answered this question in *Physics and Politics*; but it seemed to me that scientific successes in kindred fields suggested some principles which removed many of its difficulties. These are the sorts of ideas with which, under the name of 'natural selection' in physical science, we are now familiar; and as every great scientific conception tends to advance its boundaries and to be of use in solving problems not thought of when it was started, so here, what was put forward for mere animal history may, with a change of form, but an identical essence, be applied to human history. At first some objection was raised to the principle of 'natural selection' in physical science upon religious grounds; it was to be expected that so active an idea and so large a shifting of thought would seem to imperil much which men valued. But the new principle is now more and more seen to be fatal to mere outworks of religion, not to religion itself. At all events, to the sort of application I made of it, which only amounted to searching out and following up an analogy suggested by it, there was plainly no objection.

Man, being the strongest of all animals, differs from the rest: he was obliged to be his own domesticator. Law—rigid, definite, concise law—is the primary want of early mankind; that which they need above anything else, that which is requisite before they can gain anything else. Early society had to obtain a fixed law by processes of incredible difficulty. Those who surmounted that difficulty soon destroyed all those who lay in their way and were then caught in their own yoke of custom. In the great majority of cases the progress of mankind was thus arrested in its earliest shape, closely embalmed in a mummy-like imitation of its primitive existence. I endeavoured to show in what manner, and how slowly, and in how few cases this yoke or cake of custom was removed. Why do men progress? The answer seems to be that they progress when they have a certain sufficient amount of variability in their nature. Progress is only possible in those happy cases where the force of legality has gone far enough to bind the nation together, but not far enough to kill out all varieties and destroy nature's perpetual tendency to change.

In my reading of the past, in every particular state of the world, those nations which are strongest, which have military advantage, tend to prevail over the others; and in certain marked peculiarities the strongest tend to be the best. Furthermore, within every particular nation the types of character then and there most attractive tend to prevail; and the most attractive, though with exceptions, is what we call the best character. But one of the greatest impediments to the development of human character is the pain of a new ideal. Experience shows just how incredibly difficult it is to get men to encourage the principle of originality. How then did civilization come to throw off the customary disciplines and terrible sanctions that killed out of the whole society the propensities to variation which are the principle of progress?

To this question history gives a clear and remarkable answer. Over the centuries, it is that the change from the age of status to the age of choice was first made in states where the government was to a great and a growing extent a government by discussion, and where the subjects of that discussion were in some degree abstract, or, as we should say, matters of principle. It was in the small republics of Greece and Italy that the chain of custom was first broken. 'Let there be light! said Liberty. And like sunrise from the sea, Athens arose!' wrote Shelley, and his historical philosophy was in this case far more correct than is usual with him. The originality of mankind was set free where the government was to a great and a growing extent a government by discussion, and where the subjects of that discussion were in some degree matters of principle. Once the process began to operate, the advantages of a polity which admitted discussion accelerated its formation. As soon as this great step upwards is once made, the higher gifts and graces of humanity have a rapid and a definite effect on 'verifiable progress'—on progress in the narrowest, because the most universally admitted, sense of the term.

A polity of discussion not only tends to diminish our inherited defects, but also to augment a heritable excellence. Not least, it encourages imitation, tolerance and co-operation; it strengthens a subtle quality or combination of qualities singularly useful in practical life. Progressive nations are ones which can discuss exciting subjects without over-excitement. Their emergence in Europe did not depend on the eager people with an impulse to action who were victorious in the barbarous ages, but on the quiet people, the scientists and star-gazers who sat still and worked out the doctrine of chances, the most 'dreamy moonshine', without which modern life could not have existed. Ages of sedentary, quiet, thinking people were required before that noisy existence began, and without those pale preliminary students it never could have been brought into being. And nine-tenths of modern science is in this respect the same: it is the product of men whom their contemporaries thought dreamers—who were laughed at for caring for what did not concern them—who were believed to be useless. And the conclusion is plain that if there had been more such people, if the world had not laughed at those there were, if rather it had encouraged them there would have been a great accumulation of proved science ages before there was.

Success in life depends more than anything else on animated moderation, on a certain combination of energy of mind and balance of mind, hard to attain and harder to keep. And this subtle excellence is aided by all the finer graces of humanity. It is a matter of common observation that, though often separated, fine taste and fine judgment go very much together. In meta-physics both taste and judgment involve what is termed 'poise of mind', that is the power of true passiveness—the faculty of 'waiting' till the stream of impressions, whether those of life or those of art, have done all that they have to do, and cut their full type plainly upon the mind. The ill-judging and the untasteful are both over-eager; both move too quick and blur the image. The union between a subtle sense of beauty and a subtle discretion in conduct is a natural one, because it rests on the common possession of a fine power, though that union may be often disturbed.

In this quality of animated moderation, the English excel all other nations. There is an infinite deal to be laid against us, and as we are unpopular with most others, and as we are always grumbling at ourselves, there is no want of people to say it. But, after all, England is a success in the world; her career has had many faults, but still it has been a fine and winning career upon the whole. And this is on account of the exact possession of this particular quality. What is the making of a successful merchant? That he has plenty of energy, and yet that he does not go too far. And if you ask for a description of a great practical Englishman, you will be sure to have this, or something like it, 'Oh, he has plenty of go in him; but he knows when to pull up.' He may have all other defects in him; he may be coarse, he many be illiterate, he may be stupid to talk to; still this great union of spur and bridle, of energy and moderation, will remain to him.

There is no better example of this quality in English statesmen than Lord Palmerston. There are, of course, many most serious accusations to be made against him. The sort of homage with which he was regarded in the last years of his life has passed away; the spell is broken, and the magic cannot be again revived. We may think that his information was meagre, that his imagination was narrow, that his aims were short-sighted and faulty.

But though we may often object to his objects, we rarely find much to criticize in his means. 'He went', it has been said, 'with a great swing'; but he never tumbled over; he always managed to pull up 'before there was any danger'. He was an odd man to have inherited Hampden's motto *MEDIOCRIA FIRMA*; still, there was a great trace of it in him—as much, probably, as there could be in anyone of such great vivacity and buoyancy. Palmerston was not a common man, but a common man might have been cut out of him.

⁂

There is an accusation against our age that our energies are diminishing, that ordinary and average men have not the quick determination nowadays which they used to have when the world was younger; that not only do committees and parliaments no longer act with rapid decisiveness, but that no one now so acts. I hope that this is true, for it proves that the hereditary barbaric impulse to action is decaying and dying out. So far from thinking the quality attributed to us a defect, I wish that those who complain of it were far more right than I much fear they are. Still, certainly, eager and violent action is somewhat diminished, though only by a small fraction of what it ought to be. And I believe that this is in great part due, in England at least, to our government by discussion, which has fostered a general intellectual tone, a disposition to weigh evidence, a conviction that much may be said on every side of everything which the elder and more fanatic ages of the world found intolerable.

It is plain that a government by conversation multiplies good results in practical life. It enables men to see what is good; it gives them intellect enough for sufficient perception; but it does not make men all intellect; it enables them to do the good things they see to be good, as well as to see that they are good. In such a polity, a strong idiosyncratic mind, violently disposed to extremes of opinion, is soon weeded out of political life. A vigorous moderateness in mind and body is the rule of a polity which works by discussion; and, upon the whole, it is the kind of temper most suited to the active life of such a being as man in such a world as the present one. George Lewis was the perfect specimen of the temperate English administrator; he ran the War Office with a sluggish diligence, like a conveyancer poring over ancient deeds. I once visited him in his office when war with America seemed about to be declared, yet he set aside the matter to discuss the uncertainty of the physical and moral sciences.

It may be argued that there is some quality in the thought of Englishmen which makes them fashion as many, if not more, first-rate and original suggestions than nations of greater scientific culture. I believe the reason for the English originality to be that government by discussion quickens and enlivens thought all through society; that it makes people think no harm may come of thinking; that in England this force has long been operating, and so it has developed more of all kinds of people ready to use their mental energy in their own way, and not ready to use it in a despotic way. And so rare is great originality among mankind, and so great are its fruits, that this one benefit of free government probably outweighs what are in many cases its accessory evils. Of itself it justifies our saying with Montesquieu, 'Whatever be the cost of this glorious liberty, we must be content to pay it to heaven.'

CHAPTER XII

❧❧❧

Political Economy

THE changes in the nation's business and political life corresponded to changes in my own. I have lived through several
financial crises and have found myself drawn increasingly into
commercial discussions. Since the banking crisis of 1857, when
Mr Wilson first approached me to write for *The Economist*, I have
been sought out for my observations on the behaviour of the
money market and the trade cycle. Gladstone placed me in his
confidence on the management of economic policy, and since the
Conservatives returned to power I have advised the Chancellor of
the Exchequer on financing the government's debt. Such work is
a shadowy trade, requiring discretion, but someone needs to do it,
for men of business are unreliable observers; they have not yet
learned to make use of their intellect and never pause to think if
they can help it. They have a wonderful power of guessing what
is going to happen—each in his own trade; but they have never
practised in reasoning out their judgments and in supporting
their guesses by argument. They are like the lady to whom
Coleridge said, 'Madam, I accept your conclusion but you must
let me find the logic.'

Business is really a profession often requiring for its practice quite as much knowledge, and quite as much skill, as law and medicine. But men of business can no more put into words much of what guides their life than they can tell another person how to speak their language. And so the 'theory of business' leads a life of obstruction, because theorists do not see the business, and the men of business will not reason out the theories. Capitalists in a commercial nation not only do the work of foremen in superintending labour, but do the difficult work of commerce besides, which rarely stimulates reflection. The rough and vulgar structure of English commerce is the secret of its life, for it contains 'the propensity to variation', which, in the social as in the animal kingdom, is the principle of progress. But we see so much of the material fruits of commerce that we forget its mental fruits.

A mind desirous of things is careless of ideas and unacquainted with the niceties of words. Capitalists are little respected as a class because they are unrefined and often knavish. The constant levelling of our commercial houses in the democratic structure of business is unfavourable to commercial morality—the sudden millionaires of the present day hope to disguise their defects by buying old houses and hiding among aristocratic furniture. But chiefly capitalists are little respected because they are too dumb to explain in laymen's terms the complex processes by which they estimate the wants of the community and how best to supply them. What is needed is a language—and a psychology of the subtle game of finance—so that the men of business and guardians of the economy can explain the commercial process. Political economy needs to be served by art, buoyed by facts and figures.

Lombard Street, which I began in the autumn of 1870, but which, for reasons of health and other obligations, did not appear until 1873, was an attempt to illuminate the history and nature of business panics and to shed some light on the psychology of buying and selling money. I ventured to call my essay 'Lombard Street' and not the 'Money Market' because I wished to show that I meant to deal with concrete realities. A notion prevails that the money market is something so impalpable that it can only be spoken of in very abstract words, and therefore books on it must always be exceedingly difficult. But I maintain that the money market, which is the greatest combination of economical power and economical delicacy that the world has ever seen, is as concrete and real as anything else. It can be described in plain words, and it is the writer's fault if what he says is not clear.

I feared that the book would not receive a favourable reception, for it had a grounding in statistics, which, though essential to our understanding of the money market, have little charm for all but the most persevering readers. Moreover, it spoke of bankers and bill brokers in terms unlikely to be altogether pleasing to them. Nor was it likely to gratify the purest of free traders. I am not doctrinaire about the principle of laissez-faire in matters of banking and the money market. I do not belong to that uncompromising tribe of economists who condemn the intervention of government in the nation's business as a heinous crime and contrary to reason, for in an economic crisis the government has a duty to intervene in the national interest. For all its faults, *Lombard Street* was slowly matured in 'Lombard Street' itself and had the merit of being impartial in its criticism. It provided some preparatory work for the solution of problems that could only be solved statistically and was levelled at the magnates of the City, who needed some fundamental truths to be knocked into their heads to prevent them from reckless action.

As I observed nearly twenty years ago, much of the panic to which our economy is susceptible results from an over-extension of credit. Our capital is clothed in a soft web of confidence and opinion; on a sudden it may be stripped bare, and with pain to our prosperity. The mercantile community will have been unusually fortunate if during the period of rising prices it has not made great mistakes. Such a period naturally excites the sanguine and the ardent. Energy of enterprise is the life of England; our buoyant temperament drives us into action, while our solid courage is inapprehensive of fanciful risk. Sanguine investors fancy that the prosperity they see will last always, that it is only the beginning of greater prosperity. They altogether over-estimate the demand for the article they deal in, or the work they do. They all in their degree—and the ablest and the cleverest the most—work much more than they should, and trade far above their means. Every great crisis reveals the excessive speculations of many houses, which no one before suspected, and which commonly had not begun until tempted by the daily rise of price and the surrounding fever.

The good times of high prices almost always engender fraud. Credulity is the *natural* condition of man, and all people are most credulous when they are most happy. When much money has just been made, when some people are really making it, when most people think they are making it, there is an opportunity for ingenious mendacity. Almost everything will be believed for a little while, and long before discovery the worst and most adroit deceivers are geographically or legally beyond the reach of punishment. But the harm they have done weakens credit farther. In such a crisis, many of the strongest heads in England spend their minds on little else than on thinking whether other people will pay their debts. The life of Lombard Street bill brokers is almost exclusively so spent. In the City, where so many hopes are crushed every day, the 'Bull' goes on believing in his own too sanguine expectations, and the 'Bear' in his own dismal predictions. Like children who believe in fairy tales, they expect some great enchanter's wand will be triumphantly found at last, when only the hard discipline of constant disappointment can batter their credulity.

My own reading of history and my personal experience suggest that the swings of the trade cycle and the quicksand of the money market cannot be eliminated, but their ill effects might be mitigated by a more sensible policy on the part of the Bank of England, which suffers from amateurish directors and the public's lack of a clear understanding of its purposes. We have placed the exclusive custody of our entire banking reserve in the hands of a single board of directors not particularly trained for the duty, who have no particular interest above other people in keeping it undiminished—who acknowledge no obligation to keep it undiminished—who have never been told by any great statesman or public authority that they are so to keep it or that they have anything to do with it—who do not fear, and who need not fear, ruin, even if it were all gone and wasted. That such an arrangement is strange must be plain.

No country has ever been so exposed as England to a foreign demand on its banking reserve, not only because England is a large borrower from foreign nations, but also because no nation has ever had a foreign trade of such magnitude. But my recommendations to increase the Bank's gold reserve to meet future emergencies, and to respond more quickly and sensitively to drains upon it through its interest rate policy, were widely seen as undue interference by its Directors, who are little inclined to take advice from outsiders. I recall George Lewis, then Chancellor of the Exchequer, saying to a deputation of Scotch bankers who wished the Bank of England to make advances to them, 'Ah, gentlemen, if I were to interfere with the discretion of the Bank, there would be a run upon me much greater than any which there has ever been upon you.'

I recognize that the existing system of the Bank of England is too firmly established to be dramatically altered; the reforms I advocated were not meant to sweep away the existing system, but simply to achieve a more responsible policy in the management of financial crises, which will not be eradicated as long as man is a creature of the market-place. You might as well try to alter the English monarchy and substitute a republic, as to alter the present constitution of the English money market founded on the Bank of England. Nothing but a revolution would effect it, and there is nothing to cause a revolution. There is nothing for it but to make the best of our established banking system, and to work it in the best way that it is capable of. We can only use palliatives, and the point is to get the best palliative we can. *Lombard Street* was meant to suggest the best that are at our disposal.

❧❦❧

My life at the time of writing *Lombard Street* had settled into a familiar muddle, full of duties and deadlines, complaints and fatigue, which taxed my wife and troubled my friends. It was further complicated by regular trips to Langport to attend meetings of the Stuckey Bank as its Vice-Chairman and to visit my father, whose health had deteriorated after the death of my mother. In London, I now take refuge from the taxations of society at Brooks's, and latterly at the Athenaeum, where I have the added pleasure of defeating Hutton at chess. I attend the monthly meetings at the Political Economy Club, which find expression in my writings. From time to time, I also participate in the lively gatherings of the Metaphysical Society, which attempts an intellectual rapprochement between religion and science. The churchmen invited me to join as a representative of the scientific 'opposition'.

The Metaphysical Society has an illustrious membership, which includes Tennyson, Gladstone, Hutton, Morley, Mark Pattison, T. H. Huxley, Leslie Stephen, Dean Stanley and Cardinal Manning. The meetings have discussed a range of topics that have long preoccupied me, among them the theory of causation, the ethics of belief, the nature of moral principle, the personality of God and the arguments for a future life. James Anthony Froude, another of our members, remarked that if we hung together for twelve months it would be one of the most remarkable facts in history. Seven years on the 'symposium' somehow survives. We try to keep in mind Tennyson's remark at an early meeting that 'modern science ought, at any rate, to have taught us one thing—how to separate light from heat'. Some years ago, I gave a paper at the Society, 'On the Emotion of Conviction', to our group of outspoken men of diametrically opposite beliefs. It was a salutary lesson in the utility of toleration and a good dinner.

⁂

As I set to work on *Lombard Street* in September 1870, the Emperor Napoleon surrendered with an army of 80,000 to the Germans at Sedan. I received the news by telegram while having lunch at home in Wimbledon. It came as something of a shock, for the curtain had dropped on a career which I had followed with a curious fascination since my insouciant letters on the *coup d'état* twenty years earlier. Louis Napoleon's form of Caesarism was absolute government with a popular instinct, irresponsible power obtained by one man from the vague preference of the masses for a particular name. A democratic despotism is like a theocracy, it assumes its own correctness. It says: 'I am the representative of the people: I am here because I know what they wish, because I know what they should have.' Such a despotism could not permit its principles to be questioned, for all popular discussion was radically at issue with the hypothesis of Caesar's omniscience.

Along with America, France is the foreign nation which has attracted my greatest interest; its history is entwined with England's and its revolutions raised constitutional issues of the first importance. I wrote a series of articles on the Emperor's downfall and subsequent events in France. His death in Chislehurst in 1873 threw a flood of light upon his later career. It was in 1868 that he first began perceptibly to lose confidence in himself, and to desire if means might be found to transmute his Caesarism into constitutional monarchy. It is said that Bismarck's policy weighed upon his mind and disturbed his judgment. But as is now perceived, there was another cause. He had been attacked by a malady, which, besides threatening his constitution, exerted a singular power over his mind, depriving him of nervous strength, of energy, and of the capacity for resolution. As a victim of kidney stones he ceased to be able to examine details, lost his confidence in old friends, and began to indulge in the despondency which sent him in 1870 to the field a man beaten in advance. During the campaign his exertions increased his complaint so that he had no longer the energy to direct, and when at Sedan a tremendous effort might have saved him, he had not the physical power to make it.

In spite of his failure, I believe the powers of Napoleon III to have been very considerable. Though not a great administrator—a function for which he was too indolent—he was perhaps the most reflective and *in*sighted, not farsighted, of modern statesmen of France. He perceived years before other men the spell which the name of his uncle threw over the Frenchmen who had forgotten the disasters of 1815. He comprehended years before other men that the peasantry were the governing body, and would, if secured in their properties, adhere firmly to any strong executive. He understood the latent power existing in the idea of nationalities years before old diplomatists could see in it anything but a dream. He was aware of the resources which might be developed by a free trade policy before a single politician in France had realized the first principles of economic finance. Alone among French politicians he contrived to conciliate the Papacy without breaking with the Republicans, and alone among

Frenchmen he ventured to declare that England was the best ally France could have.

It is too early yet to discuss frankly the character of the Emperor, but as we have indicated the greatest of his mental powers—cool and broad political insight—we may also indicate the greatest of his mental defects as a politician. He was incapable, almost beyond precedent, of securing competent agents. He never discovered a great soldier. He never found a great statesman. He never secured a great financier. Mere indolence does not explain it, for amidst the 500,000 officials employed in France it does not take very much trouble to pick out a few strong men; and mere carelessness does not explain it, for the Emperor was well aware how badly he was sometimes served. It is difficult, considering the wealth of intellect in France, to doubt that the Emperor had the foible of men whose position is slightly uncertain, that he was jealous of very able persons, particularly if they were statesmen. Such men, if Frenchmen, are anxious to make their personality felt, and the Emperor could not bear that any personality should be felt except his own, lest it attract the regard of a population accustomed to raise its favourites to the top.

Louis Napoleon was not the Lord's anointed but the people's agent—a Benthamite despot. In his heyday, he had a mind daring in ideas, recoiling before the hazardous, shrinking from the irrevocable, and certain not to venture on the desperate. There is no doubt that, if he had remained quiet, the peasantry and the army would have remained true to him; but he could not with his morbid sense of insecurity, irritated to madness by disease, believe the truth, and therefore he fell. We shall, as time goes on and memoirs appear, know much more of Napoleon III than we do now, but we believe, when all is known, the world will decide that his grand merit as a politician was a certain clearness of insight, and that his grand defect was self-distrust, leading to jealous impatience of capacities unlike or superior to his own. To declare him a great man may be impossible in the face of his failures, but to declare him a small one is ridiculous.

❦

In the autumn of 1873, after the completion of *Lombard Street*, Eliza and I made a pilgrimage to Metz and the battlefield of Gravelotte, then on to Strasbourg, Freiburg, Innsbruck, Munich, Augsburg and other towns, large and small, marked by historical associations or beautiful scenery. I had become weary of the constant journeys to and from Wimbledon, and on our return we rented a house in Rutland Gate before settling permanently in Queen's Gate Place. I chose a room on the third floor as my study, where I could work away from the fuss of the front door. William Morris's firm took charge of the interior decoration, which was an adventure for practical people with little regard for extravagant living. From time to time, I met Morris in Bloomsbury to choose papers and tiles, where we talked of poetry as well as furnishings. He has decided views as to the morality or immorality of different colours and designs. An autocrat when it comes to taste, he composed the drawing room as he would an ode and designed a remarkably moral blue damask silk for the curtains.

❦

Lombard Street and daily contact with the world of business furthered my interest in economic thought, which the present agricultural crisis has intensified. Consequently, I set my mind to writing a series of economic studies, which emerged out of the inquiry begun in *Physics and Politics*. What had grown upon the world was a certain matter-of-factness, for which science and business were largely responsible. A new world of inventions—of railways and of telegraphs—had come into being which we could not help seeing; a new world of ideas was in the air which affected us, though we did not see it. A full estimate of the effects of these seen and unseen changes would require a great book, and I was sure I could not write it; but I thought I might usefully, in a few papers, show how, upon one or two great points, the new ideas were modifying two old sciences—politics and political economy.

The first thing to be done for English political economy is to straighten its aim. So long as writers on it do not see clearly, and as readers do not see at all, the limits of what they are analysing, the result will not satisfy either. The science will seem what to many minds it seems now, proved perhaps, but proved *in nubibus*; true, no doubt, somehow and somewhere, but that somewhere a *terra incognita* and that somehow an unknown quantity. As help in this matter I proposed to take the principal assumptions of political economy one by one, to show roughly where each is true and where it is not. We would then find that our political economy is not a questionable thing of unlimited extent, but a most certain and useful thing of limited extent. By marking the frontier of our property we would learn its use, and we would have a positive and reliable basis for estimating its value.

It was my intention to make a contribution which would link political economy to the real world and lift it from the siege of the social sciences. But I could not hurry my mind over so important a work, and I feared it would never be finished except in pieces. The initial proposal was to write three volumes, including one on celebrated political economists, but my illness and commitments confined me to an inquiry into the foundations and history of economic thought, and secondly into the stages of actual economic development. I completed sketches of Malthus, 'a mild pottering person' who, in spite of himself, will always be connected to the revolution in economic thought, and Ricardo, the true founder of abstract political economy. But I failed to finish an estimate of Mill and laboured to finish 'The Postulates of Political Economy', which appeared in the *Fortnightly* at the beginning of 1876. In fact, I completed only two postulates, the transferability of labour and the transferability of capital; a few unfinished fragments reside in my desk as a reproach.

My countrymen will take little notice of my failings and omissions, for no real English gentleman, in his secret soul, was ever sorry for the death of a political economist; he is much more likely to be sorry for his life. There is an idea that an economist has something to do with statistics; or that he is a person who writes upon 'value'. He may be useful as drying machines are useful; but the notion of crying about him is absurd. You might as well cry at the death of a cormorant. Indeed, how he can die is very odd. You would think a man who could digest all that arid matter, who really preferred 'sawdust with butter', who liked the tough subsistence of rigid formulae, might defy by intensity of internal constitution all stomachic or lesser diseases. However, economists do die, and people say that the dryness of the Sahara is caused by a deposit of similar bones.

Given the aridity of political economy, its position lies rather dead in the public mind, notwithstanding the triumphs of English commerce. Younger men either do not study it, or do not feel that it comes home to them or matches with their most living ideas. New sciences have come up in the last few years with new modes of investigation, and they want to know what is the relation of economic science, as their fathers held it, to these new thoughts and these new instruments. They ask, often hardly knowing it: will this 'science', as it claims to be, harmonise with what we now know to be sciences, or bear to be tried as we now try sciences? And they are not sure of the answer.

Political economy is essentially a theory which assumes the principal facts which make commerce possible, and as is the way of an abstract science it isolates and simplifies them: it detaches them from the confusion with which they are mixed. And it deals too with the men who carry on that commerce, and who make it possible. It assumes a sort of human nature such as we see everywhere around us; but it simplifies that human nature, for it looks at one part of it only. Dealing with matters of 'business', it assumes that man is actuated only by motives of business. It assumes that every man who makes anything, makes it for money, that he always makes that which brings him in most at least cost, and that he will make it in the way that will produce most and cost least. It assumes that every man who buys, buys with his whole heart, and that he who sells, sells with his whole heart, each wanting to gain all possible advantage. Of course, we know that men are not like this, but we assume it for simplicity's sake, as a hypothesis. And this deceives many excellent people, for from deficient education they have very indistinct ideas of what an abstract science is.

English political economists have been content to remain in the 'abstract', and to shrink from concrete notions, because they could not but feel that many of the most obvious phenomena of many nations did not look much like their abstractions. In the societies with which the science is really concerned, an almost infinite harvest of verification was close at hand, ready to be gathered in; and because it has not been used, much confidence in the science has been lost, and it is thought 'to be like the stars which give no good light because they are so high'. This reasoning implies that the boundaries of an abstract science like political economy are arbitrary. All abstractions are arbitrary; they are more or less convenient fictions made by the mind for its own purposes. An abstract idea means a concrete fact or set of facts minus something thrown away. The fact or set of facts was made by nature; but how much you will throw aside and how much you will keep for consideration you settle for yourself.

And this brings out the inherent difficulty of the subject—a difficulty which no other science presents in equal magnitude. Years ago, I heard Mr Cobden say at a meeting of the Anti-Corn

Law League that 'political economy was the highest study of the human mind, for the physical sciences required by no means so hard an effort'. An orator cannot be expected to be precise, and of course political economy is in no sense the highest study of the mind—there are others which are much higher, for they are concerned with things much nobler than wealth or money. Nor is it true that the effect of mind which political economy requires is nearly as great as that needed for the more abstruse theories of physical science. Nevertheless, what Mr Cobden meant had—as usual with his first-hand mind—a great fund of truth. He meant that political economy—effectual political economy, political economy which in complex problems succeeds—is a very difficult thing; something altogether more abstruse and difficult, as well as more conclusive, than that which many of those who rush in upon it have a notion of.

Political economy is an abstract science which labours under special hardships. The mere idea of such a science has evidently never crossed the minds of many able writers, and persons who have given but slight consideration to the matter are much puzzled. Its critics are often uncultured moralists, who see all manner of reasonings framed, and of conclusions drawn, apparently about subjects with which morality itself is concerned deeply—about, say, industry and wealth, population and poverty—and they never dream that there is anything peculiar about these conclusions. They apply the 'rules of morality' to them at once; they ask 'is the argument B true of good persons? Would not conclusion C augment wickedness?' In fact, the economic writers under consideration did not mean—and rightly did not mean—to deal with ethics at all. They only evolved a hypothesis; they did not intend that their arguments should be thought to be taken from real life, or that their conclusions should be, as they stood, applied to real life. They dealt not with man, the moral being, but with man, the money-making animal.

Those who are conversant with the abstractions of political economy are usually without a true contact with its facts; those who are in contact with its facts have usually little sympathy with and little cognizance of its abstractions. Literary men who write about it are constantly using what a great teacher calls 'unreal words'. That is, they are using expressions with which no complete vivid picture corresponds. They are like physiologists who have never dissected; like astronomers who have never seen the stars; and, in consequence, just when they seem to be reasoning at their best, their knowledge of the facts falls short. Their primitive picture fails them, and their deduction altogether misses the mark—sometimes, indeed, goes astray so far that those who live and move among the facts boldly say that they cannot comprehend 'how anyone can talk such nonsense'.

The necessity of political economy is that we must borrow its words from common life, and therefore from a source where they are not used accurately, and cannot be used accurately. When we come to reason strictly on the subjects to which they relate, we must always look somewhat precisely to their meaning; and the worst is that it will not do, if you are writing for the mass of men, even of educated men, to use words always in the same sense. Common words are so few, that if you tie them down to one meaning they are not enough for your purpose; they do their work in common life because they are in a state of incessant slight variation, meaning one thing in one discussion and another a little different in the next. If we were really to write an invariable nomenclature in a science where we have so much to say of so many things as we have in political economy, we must invent new terms, like the writers on other sciences. Anyone who tries to express varied meanings on complex things with a scanty vocabulary of fastened senses will find that his style grows cumbrous without being accurate.

In the centenary of *The Wealth of Nations*, I diverted my attention to an appraisal of Adam Smith, who was to feature in my proposed volume of portraits of economists. He completed his great work in 1776 and thus our political economy has reached an important anniversary. In that time it has had a wonderful effect. The life of almost everyone in England—perhaps of everyone—is different and better in consequence of *The Wealth of Nations*. The whole commercial policy of the country is not so much founded on it as instinct with it. Ideas which are paradoxes everywhere else in the world are accepted axioms here as a result of it. No other form of political philosophy has ever had one-thousandth part of the influence on us; its teachings have settled down into the common sense of the nation and have become irreversible.

What Adam Smith achieved was much like the rough view of the first traveller who discovers a country: he saw some great outlines well, but he mistook others and left out much. Nothing beforehand—nothing if we look at the matter with the eyes, say, of the year 1770—could have seemed more unlikely than that Adam Smith should have succeeded in such an achievement. Political economy is, above all things, a theory of business, and if ever there was an eminent man who pre-eminently was not a man of business it was Adam Smith. He was a bookish student who never made a sixpence, who was unfit for all sorts of affairs, and whose absence of mind is hardly credible. If the townsmen of Kirkcaldy—the little place where *The Wealth of Nations* was written—had been told to select the townsman who was most unlikely to tell this world how to make money, most likely they would have selected Adam Smith, whose writings have, in fact, caused more money to be made, and prevented more money from being wasted, than those of any other author.

As far as England is concerned, most of the legislative effects of the work of Adam Smith are complete. He thought the adop tion of a free trade legislation as unlikely as the creation of a

'Utopia', but yet it has been established. The fetters in which pre-existing laws bound our commerce have been removed, and the result is that we possess the greatest, the most stable, and the most lucrative commerce which the world has ever seen. Deep as Adam Smith's conviction of the truth of his principles, the history of England for the last thirty years would have been almost inconceivable to him. Thirty years ago Carlyle and Arnold had nearly convinced the world of the irrecoverable poverty of our lower classes. The 'condition of England question', as they termed it, was bringing us fast to ruin. But, in fact, we were on the eve of the great prosperity. And it was to the repeal of the Corn Laws in 1846, and to the series of changes of which this was the type, and the most important, that we owe this wonderful contrast.

Many persons are now deterred from reading *The Wealth of Nations* by the dullness of modern books on political economy, but most of it really consists of some of the most striking and graphic writing in the language. And its defect, like that of several other great works of the eighteenth century, is rather that it tries to make its subject more interesting than it ought to be, and not to dwell on the dull standpoints of the truth, though these are often the most important parts of all. But perhaps for its peculiar time and purpose its defect was almost a merit. It gained a hearing from the mass of mankind, who always think they ought to be able to understand even the most complex subjects with little effort, and so brought home approximate truth to those most concerned in its application. A student familiar with abstractions may prefer teaching like Ricardo's, which begins in dry principles and goes with unabbreviated reasoning to conclusions that are as dry. But such students are very rare. Teaching like Adam Smith's, imperfect and external as from its method it is, vitally changes the minds and maxims of thousands to whom an abstract treatise is intolerable.

Adam Smith will always be quoted as the great authority on anti-protectionism—as the man who first told the world the truth so that the world could learn and believe it. And besides this great practical movement, he started a great theoretical one also, though he never seems aware that he is dealing with what we should call an abstract science at all. On one side his teaching created Cobden and Bright, on another it rendered possible Ricardo and Mill. He is the founder of that analysis of the 'great commerce' which in England we now call political economy, and which, dry, imperfect and unfinished as it is, will be thought by posterity one of the most valuable and peculiar creations of English thought. So much theory and so much practice have perhaps never sprung from a single thinker. In the popular mind, free trade has become almost as much Adam Smith's subject as the war of Troy was Homer's.

Fortunate in many things, Adam Smith was above all things fortunate in his age. Commerce had become far more striking, far more world-wide than it ever was before, and it needed an effectual explainer. On a strong-headed man of business, semi-insincere exposition produces no effect. A vigorous Scotchman like Smith, with the hard-headedness and the abstraction of his country, trained in England and familiar with France, was the species of man best fitted to explain political economy. He believed, as it has been justly said, that 'there is a Scotchman inside every man', and he took up his subject in a solid straight-forward way, such as he knew would suit the Glasgow merchants with whom he had once lived. He found the words for his time and his successors now speak his language.

The fame which *The Wealth of Nations* has obtained, and its special influence, did not begin in his lifetime, and he had no notion of it. Nor would he perhaps have quite appreciated it if he had, for he probably did not know the exceeding merit of his work and preferred the more learned parts of his writings, which are now obsolete, and the more refined parts, which are now seen to have little value. Political economy—the study of man as the man of business—was only a small part of his capacious mind, which included his great scheme of the origin and history of all cultivation, which he never completed. 'I meant to have done more,' he said in a melancholy way at the end of life. As happens to so many men, though scarcely ever on so grand a scale, he aimed at one sort of reputation and attained another. Like Saul, to use Lord Bacon's illustration, he 'went in search of his father's asses, and he found a kingdom'.

CHAPTER XIII

Valediction

M Y last review, on Lord Althorp, appeared in the *Fortnightly* in November 1876. I was drawn to him because he recalled my childhood memories of the 1832 Reform Act; a man picturesquely out of place; wise with the solid wisdom of rural England; popular and useful; content to end his days in the country away from the maelstrom of politics. I have since continued to write for *The Economist* but am now facing my final deadline, for which I am ill prepared but seeking to be stoical. My recent cold has brought on a severe attack of the lungs and has weakened my heart, and the medications no longer have any effect. Shortly after my fifty-first birthday, I rose from bed to make my will. I think Hutton must have the evil eye, for he visited some days ago and complimented me on my appearance. I have been sickening ever since. With Easter approaching and my ailing father needing attention, Eliza and I set off on the familiar journey to Herd's Hill, the place of so many of my fondest memories.

Like Lord Althorp, my life has been picturesquely out of place; a man from a quiet county transported to the clamour of the capital, an amateur on the stage of the professional. My nomadic mind has never settled on a single subject; waiting for truth to come, I have followed the truth that came my way. My moderate Liberalism shrinks from difficult dogma and imperious superstition, from facile abstraction and precipitous action. It has more to do with tolerance, steady judgment and genial enjoyment than advocacy or creed. Without a craving for power or renown, I am detached in the face of desire and conscious of life's absurdities. I am 'cast in an antique mould', and in my conversation with the disconsolate world, the customary and familiar have seemed to me the most endearing, and the endearing the most probable.

'Old things need not be therefore true,'
O brother men, nor yet the new;
Ah, still awhile, the old thought retain,
And yet consider it again!

I am not destined to enjoy the quiet pleasures of ambition spent. But I will not suffer the indignities of old age, nor, like Aeneas in the throat of Hades, sink into Stygian gloom. Like Gibbon contemplating the barbarous state of most humanity, I have drawn a high prize in the lottery of life. I was born in a free country to an honourable and prosperous family and have travelled back and forth between the worlds of literature and commerce; I have conversed with poets and merchant princes, farmers and ploughmen, scholars and statesmen, clergymen and scientists; and in this coming and going I have found sagacity and stupidity at every turn. In life, I have sought to find a delicate balance—a *centrality* of mind—which is the reward of an educated man with an experiencing nature. In my writing, I have sought to encourage a greater communion between literature and commerce; to restrain our reckless enterprise through culture and common sense; to give expression to a philosophy of equanimity; to translate the truths discovered by the dead into the language of the living.

As the lead in this deathbed drama, the passing hours are poignant and bewildering. My Aunt Emma plays nurse and relieves my fidgets with games of cribbage. Yesterday, Eliza sat by my side, cutting the leaves of a new copy of *Rob Roy*, which I so enjoyed as a boy. Dr Liddon from Taunton visited; he reminded me of Mrs Gaskell's storied physician, who said to Mr Hale, as he sat by the deathbed of his wife, that he should have faith in the immortality of the soul which no disease could touch. We long to hold firmly to beliefs which have been formed in childhood, not least the vague sense of eternal continuity which is always about the mind. In my own uncertain faith, I have wished to believe that the soul survives the body; the tenets of religion make it harder to live but easier to die. Yet the necessity of death does not reconcile us to it, nor teach us how to die. Since childhood, anxious about my troubled mother, I have sought to avoid lifting Shelley's 'painted veil' for fear of the chasm below; but now in the fading light, as I slip into insubstantial dream, it is being lifted for me . . .

Index

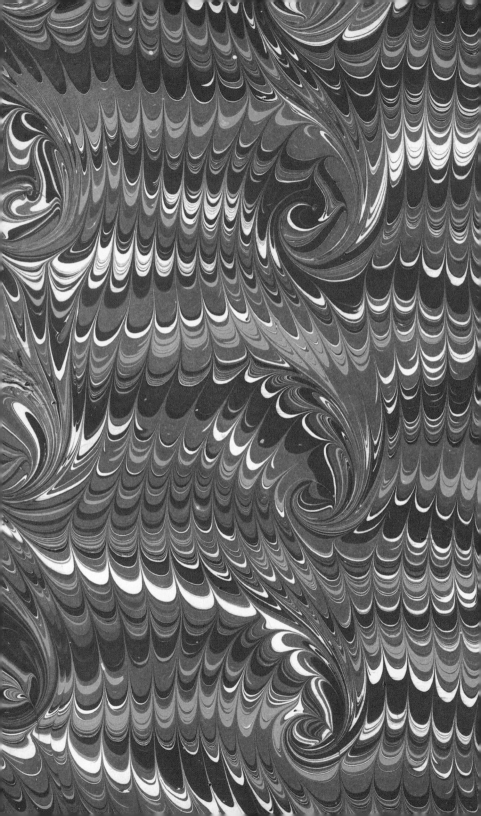